a
flash
in the
pan

simple, speedy, stovetop recipes

JOHN WHAITE

Photography by Nassima Rothacker
Kyle Books

For my scruffy boys

An Hachette UK Company
www.hachette.co.uk

First published in Great Britain in 2019 by
Kyle Books, an imprint of
Octopus Publishing Group Limited
Carmelite House
50 Victoria Embankment
London EC4Y 0DZ
www.kylebooks.co.uk

ISBN: 978 1 91423 955 7

Distributed in the US by Hachette Book Group, 1290 Avenue of the Americas,
4th and 5th Floors, New York, NY 10104

Distributed in Canada by Canadian Manda Group, 664 Annette St.,
Toronto, Ontario, Canada M6S 2C8

Publisher: Joanna Copestick
Commissioning Editor: Sophie Allen
Editorial Assistant: Sarah Kyle
Design: Paul Atkins
Photography: Nassima Rothacker
Food styling: Nicole Herft
Props styling: Nicole Herft
Production: Allison Gonsalves

A Cataloguing in Publication record for this title is available from the British Library

Printed and bound in Czechia

10 9 8 7 6 5 4 3 2

contents

Introduction

The pan, in most kitchens, is an auspicious symbol – an emblem of culinary opportunity for every home cook. We rack our brains at lunchtime to invoke ideas for the evening's dinner. The image of a hot, smoking pan serves as a life raft to carry us through the working day. A dear friend admitted that on returning home from work, the pan will go onto the hob before she's even foraged the fridge or rustled through her cupboards to concoct supper. While that isn't an action I'd recommend – unless you want a roomful of smoke by the time you've peeled your first onion – for her, merely heating a pan signals safety and homeliness. The sentimental value of that piece of formed metal balances with, if not outweighs, its basic function. Whether it's an heirloom cast-iron skillet, scrubbed clean and oiled by generations of a devoted dynasty, or the pan that fills an empty new house with the inaugural scent of home, the raw concept of the pan – metal on heat – has evolved alongside us into an indispensable part of modern day life. That story began a million years ago.

In the depths of the Wonderwerk Cave in South Africa, scientists discovered charred bone fragments and ash – evidence, some say, that our forefathers started to cook food on fire a million years ago. All it may have taken is for one member of an earlier clan, while ravaging a piece of meat, to have dropped a morsel into the fire. In the shadows that danced across the cave walls, this famished prehistoric being plucked the meat from the fire, sacrificing not a bite of the precious meal, and was enlightened by the improved flavour and texture. It's not hard to believe, is it, that the discovery of cooked meat could supersede the lustre that raw meat once had? Other scientific theories contest that timeframe of ancient cookery, and suggest a more recent use of fire for food from evidence of human-controlled fires in Israel – still a good 250,000–400,000 years ago.

It may take just one fleeting glance at a frenzy of lager louts in the local pub to question the modern-day human's anatomical advances over prehistoric man, but it has nonetheless been argued that our anatomy began its evolution to the current advanced state at the advent of cookery. No longer were we forced to spend most of the day eating raw foods. We were able to more quickly derive nutrition from cooked foods. As a result, our guts shrunk and our brains grew (until the advent of draft lager, that is).

It was only hundreds of thousands of years later that the human race began to cook with pots. As far as we currently know, pottery was first used for cooking in East Asia between 10,000 and 20,000 years ago. Tests carried out on pots found in Japan suggested that these ancient vessels were used to cook aquatic creatures. Imagine the first sip of a fish chowder – albeit of rudimentary preparation – after a lifetime of charred meat. What an awakening!

With the passage of time, more cookware emerged from human invention, with copper pans appearing around 5000 years ago in ancient Mesapotamia – and they're still very much in fashion today. In the late 19th century, cast-iron skillets arrived in America and, somewhere between then and now, a more diverse range of cookware was born. A range that we idolise and collect, as new trends oscillate in and out of life.

You might expect a bigger brain and a more advanced body to be a good thing, but as a result of these steps forward, we now have much more to do other than hunt, gather, and cook. We leave our caves for most of the day to fulfil roles, to earn a crust. The curse of our modern-day anatomies means we have to cram more into our lives, and cookery, for many, is sacrificed. But it does not have to be. In the Western world, so much emphasis is put onto a hearty meal slow cooked in the oven – it often forms the paradigm of a healthy, happy family. That's no longer a reality, and as much as I lament the lack of long, laid back family dinners, I equally rejoice the opportunities to be found in a more fast-paced kitchen environment, where delicious meals can be rustled up without an oven; just pans and a hob are all that you need to feed your tribe. You only need to look at some East Asian cultures where woks and pots replace oven cookery to be filled with confidence that you can create superb foods with just a pan and heat – convenience food, with class.

The problem with convenience food, or at least our view of it, is that it has grown to mean something very different from the contents of this book. We call junk food convenient; packet sandwiches and microwave meals are convenient; expensive salads, for which, if you ate daily, you'd need to remortgage your home, are convenient. But are they fulfilling? Occasionally, yes, they can be. I don't know about you, but I for one would much rather cook something myself for my little family (just two hairy blokes and a scruffy hound).

Of course, speedy cookbooks have been done before, but most of them require so much bloody equipment. Not all of us has a blender, a food processor, and a gang of home economists to wash up behind the scenes. Speedy food doesn't need to be complicated. It mustn't be - just a flash in the pan, and no real trickery. Knife skills help, of course; though there really is no expectation on you to chop like Gordon Ramsay on a sugar high. Home cookery shouldn't command expertise or razor-sharp agility. Just enjoy these recipes in full confidence that they can be cooked in under 45 minutes.

From our ancestors who might have spent 6–9 hours a day chewing raw food to sustain their bodies (though some days I'd love nothing more than a 6-hour feast),

we have domesticated the flames and tamed the wildness of fire, enabling a delicious dinner in 30-45 minutes.

But we owe that, really, to our ancestors; although that image of a naked, bristly crowd huddled around a cave fire seems a far cry from the convenience of our domestic cookery today, the two are inextricably moored. The simplicity of our modern-day cooking has taken millions of years of development, and we can rejoice that now with a quick flash in the pan.

speed sweet speed

sugar high note

Sugar High Note

We've come a long way. Meals are no longer solely a means for survival, but are now tailored to our pleasure receptors. The basic order in which a meal is eaten is a method of preordaining happy memories. Whether at home or in the swankiest of restaurants we follow a template procedure of starter, main and dessert. You might think this is just because we need order and organisation: patterns of regularity upon which we can rail the fickle carriage of life. But you'd be wrong. It's all about navigating toward a happy ending. And happy endings make happy memories. As Shakespeare wrote, 'All's well that ends well'.

I write this chapter introduction the day after a friend's wedding. When I recall the meal, I first smile with glee at the dessert: a trio of sorbet, brownie and steamed pudding. It was a great meal. But on deeper pondering, I then remember the pork: dry. I recall the starter being okay, maybe, definitely too small. I cringe at the forced and awkward conversation with strangers who were so inconveniently plonked behind the centrepieces. But that doesn't matter, because the meal ended on a high. The seconds it took me to snaffle the sweet far outweighed, in retrospect, the hours of waiting around and forced conversation. The day itself ended with such a fun moment with my friends that all the mundanities you'd expect of a wedding were obliterated. In psychology, it's referred to as 'duration neglect' – the idea that it doesn't matter for how long pain is suffered, so long as the pain ends on a happier note.

But can we say that in prefabricating memories from a particularly tailored order of service, we are truly living in the moment? Aren't we just worrying, unnecessarily, about the future reflections of a moment, rather than just living in it?

Putting all of the psychology aside, quite simply, I'm opening this book with dessert not to be flippant, but because of something a friend said to me in the canteen of our primary school when we were just six years old. As I drove my fork into the crispy, nature-defying golden potato croquette, I noticed my friend Kay was starting with her rice pudding and jam. I didn't need to ask; my glance was enough to draw her answer. 'Why save the best till last? Someone may steal it, or it might go cold.' Wise words from a six-year-old.

I start this meal with dessert.

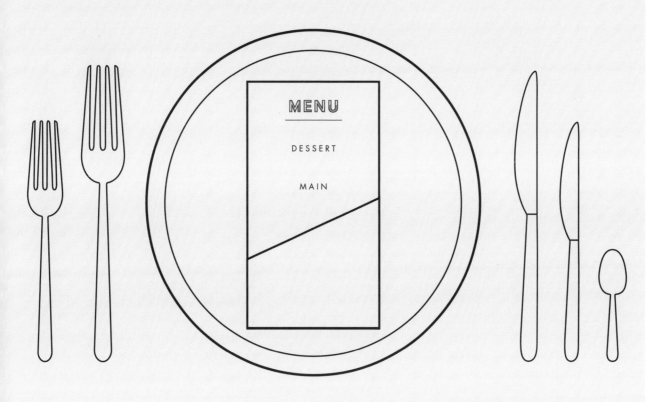

MENU

DESSERT

MAIN

Rhubarb and Matcha Eton Mess

Matcha, green tea in its powder form, is delicious in baking. Its slightly ferric, vegetal flavour, when sweetened, reminds me of rich tea biscuits dunked into very strong tea – a morning treat with which my grandma would awaken me when I was a lad. Surprisingly, it couples beautifully with stewed rhubarb. Make sure you get pure matcha powder – some supermarkets do sell it, but it'll be a darn sight cheaper online.

Serves 4

400g (14oz) rhubarb, cut into
1cm (½in) slices
100g (3½oz) caster sugar
300ml (10fl oz) double cream

½ tsp matcha powder, plus extra to sprinkle
6 meringue nests
200g (7oz) Greek yogurt

Put the rhubarb and caster sugar into a medium saucepan with a splash of water – no more than a couple of tablespoons. Set over a medium-high heat and allow the rhubarb to release its juices and cook down until just softened – don't let it get too mushy. Remove from the heat, transfer to a bowl and pop into the fridge to cool down quickly.

Put the cream and matcha powder into a mixing bowl. Whip the cream to soft, floppy peaks which reluctantly hold their shape but do so on the promise that they'll disappear if you so much as look at them in the wrong way. Crush three of the meringue nests and fold them into the cream, along with the yogurt.

When the rhubarb mixture is cool, fold it into the whipped cream, being careful not to allow the streaks of pinkish green to disappear – this is merely marbling, not combining. If you're using individual bowls rather than a huge trifle bowl, divide the mixture among them. Otherwise, scoop it into the trifle bowl. Coarsely crush the remaining three meringue nests and scatter them over the top of the Eton mess. Finish with a light dusting of matcha powder.

Apple, Panettone and Caramelised Walnut Panzanella

This is a sweet version of the classic Italian savoury salad, made with Panettone instead of stale bread, and with apples and nuts instead of tomatoes. I love a dessert that is presented like a salad, to be scooped up and eaten without pomp or etiquette. Not only does this deliver in flavour – which should be fairly obvious when looking at the ingredients – but the textures are out of this world.

Serves 4

100g (3½oz) walnuts
50g (1¾oz) caster sugar
300g (10½oz) stale panettone, cut into 2cm (1in) dice
1 Granny Smith apple

1 Braeburn apple
50g (1¾oz) unsalted butter
125g (4½oz) clotted cream
1 tbsp Calvados
1 tbsp runny honey

Set a large frying pan over a high heat. Once the pan is hot, add the walnuts and toss for a minute to toast. Move the walnuts to one side of the pan and add the sugar to the other side in a thin layer. Allow the sugar to melt into a golden caramel – stir it if it starts to burn – then stir through the walnuts until they're well coated. Tip onto a chopping board (make sure it's heatproof) and allow to cool and harden.

Wash out the pan, then return it to a high heat. Once the pan is hot, add the panettone cubes and fry, tossing once or twice, until slightly golden and crispy. Tip the toasted panettone into a large mixing bowl.

Core and quarter each apple, then slice each quarter into three. Return the pan to a high heat and add the butter. Once the butter melts, sizzles, then stops sizzling, reduce the heat to medium-high and add the apples. Fry, tossing frequently, for 10 minutes or so, until the apples are softened and lightly caramelised but retain their shape. Add the apples to the bowl with the bread and toss together.

Roughly chop the caramelised walnuts and toss them with the apples and panettone, then pour them onto a large serving plate. Dollop spoonfuls of the clotted cream randomly over the top, then drizzle with the Calvados and honey.

Sour Cherry and Mahlab Welsh Cakes

Welsh cakes, like scones, are the epitome of resourceful baking. With just a few pantry ingredients something wholesome and satiating can be rustled up. My version, while mostly similar to the original in form and texture, diverts from tradition with the use of mahlab and sour cherries. Mahlab is the dried pit of a wild cherry and is used across eastern Mediterranean countries in savoury and sweet dishes. Its flavour is like a muted amaretto – as though an almond ghost has floated through the dish. It's readily available online, so I beg you to give these a try exactly to the recipe.

250g (9oz) self-raising flour,
    plus extra for dusting
Pinch of fine sea salt
1 tbsp mahlab powder
75g (2¾oz) caster sugar,
    plus a little extra for sprinkling

120g (4¼oz) unsalted butter,
    cubed, plus 15g (½oz) for frying
80g (3oz) dried sour cherries,
    roughly chopped
1 large egg
3 tbsp amaretto

Makes 16–20

In a mixing bowl, toss together the flour, salt, mahlab and caster sugar. Add the butter and rub it into the dried ingredients as though you were making a pastry or crumble – just flick it between the pads of your first two fingers and thumbs, until the mixture resembles inelegant breadcrumbs. Toss the sour cherries through the mixture. Make a well in the centre then add the egg and amaretto. With a butter knife, cut the wet ingredients into the dry ingredients until everything starts to clump together, at which point it's best to get your hands in there and briefly knead until a smooth dough forms. As soon as you have a smooth dough, stop working it.

Dust the worktop with flour and roll out the dough until it is about 1cm thick. Cut out as many discs as you can using a 6cm cookie cutter – though if you're not fussed about quantity, use the rim of a wine glass. Whatever you use, make sure you swirl it in flour before cutting to stop the dough sticking. Ball up the offcuts, re-roll and cut.

Heat a large, deep-sided frying or sauté pan over a medium heat. Add the 15g (½oz) butter to the pan and swirl to coat, then pop in as many Welsh cakes as possible – don't crowd the pan too much. If you start at 12 o'clock and work your way around, you'll always remember which one went into the pan first. Fry on one side for 3–4 minutes until deeply golden brown, then flip and fry on the other side for a further 3–4 minutes.

Put the hot Welsh cakes onto a cooling rack and sprinkle with a little caster sugar. These are delicious served warm, but will still satisfy the most discerning of taste buds after a day or two, if kept nestled in an airtight tin.

S'mores Sundae

S'mores (an abbreviation of the recipe title Some Mores) are an American camping classic. Nestled together upon rocks before a campfire, campers hold marshmallows above the fire until they become burnished on the outside and molten on the inside. They are then sandwiched with a slab of chocolate between Graham crackers – in Lancashire, we'd probably call that a chocolate and marshmallow biscuit butty. This recipe is a sundae version of that combination, crowned, of course, with toasted Swiss meringue. Graham crackers are pretty specialist here in the UK, so I've opted for the next best thing: the digestive.

Makes 4

For the chocolate sauce
400g (14oz) can
    condensed milk
150g (5oz) dark chocolate
    (70% cocoa solids),
    broken into chunks

For the meringue
2 large egg whites
120g (4½oz)
    caster sugar

To assemble
100g (3½oz) digestive biscuits
    or Graham Crackers
8 small scoops
    vanilla ice cream
8 small scoops
    chocolate ice cream
4 cherries, to serve

Make sure you get the ice cream out of the fridge at the start of this recipe. There's nothing worse than ice cream that's so hard to scoop it gives you a strained wrist!

For the chocolate sauce, put the condensed milk and chocolate into a medium saucepan and set over a low-medium heat. Allow the chocolate to melt into the condensed milk until you have a thick, smooth sauce, stirring occasionally. Decant into a small jug or bowl.

Don't bother to clean the saucepan, just fill it a quarter full with hot water and set it over a high heat. Once the water boils, reduce the heat to a simmer. Put the egg whites and sugar into the heatproof bowl and set it over the water. Whisk constantly with the hand-held electric whisk until the meringue is thick and glossy. When it gets to that stage, remove the bowl from the heat and continue whisking until cool – this will take between 5 and 10 minutes, but it's no hardship. It's also important that if at any time you stop whisking, the bowl must be removed from above the water, otherwise the egg whites will scramble.

To assemble, crumble the biscuits into the bottom of each sundae glass. Top those with a scoop of vanilla ice cream, and try to flatten the ice cream out a little so that it fills the diameter of the glass. Top that with a generous layer of the chocolate sauce, then a layer of chocolate ice cream, again, pressing it down as best you can. Finish off a dreamy dollop of meringue. If you have a chef's blowtorch, by all means torch the meringue, if not, eat merrily in full confidence that this is still just as decadent. Serve with a cherry on top.

speed sweet speed

Butterscotch and Pecan Marshmallow Popcorn Bites

Never did a title more perfectly represent the delicacy; the title here is a mouthful, and so are these chewy, moreish bites. They are kind of like posh krispie cakes – the stickier, chewier cousin.

60g (2¼oz) salted popcorn	1 tbsp water	Makes 12
75g (2¾oz) pecans	200g (7oz) dark chocolate (60–70%	
60g (2¼oz) salted butter	cocoa solids), roughly chopped	
75g (2¾oz) dark brown muscovado sugar	Sunflower oil, for greasing (optional)	
150g (5oz) mini marshmallows	Sea salt flakes	

Put the popcorn into a large mixing bowl. Set a medium saucepan over a high heat. Once the pan is hot, add the pecans and toast, tossing occasionally, for a minute or so until the nuts fill the air with a light aroma. Chop the nuts roughly and put them into the bowl with the popcorn.

Return the pan to the heat and add the butter, allowing it to melt and sizzle. Once the butter has completely melted, add the sugar and stir until the butter and sugar are just about mixed together – it will look fairly split for a short while. Reduce the heat to medium and add the marshmallows and water. Stir for a minute or two until the marshmallows melt completely and you have a very thick but very smooth – and I'm sorry for this description – goo. Pour the mixture over the popcorn and pecans, along with a pinch of sea salt flakes, and stir to combine. It'll be fairly stiff, but just keep at it until everything is reasonably mixed. Leave to cool for a few minutes.

Meanwhile, fill the same pan (no need to clean it out) with about 2cm depth of hot tap water, and set it over a high heat. Put the chocolate into a small heatproof bowl. Reduce the heat under the pan to medium and set the bowl over the steaming water. Allow the chocolate to melt, stirring occasionally. Once melted, remove the pan from the heat.

Divide the popcorn mixture into 12 and roll each portion into balls. These will be so sticky that at one point along the way you may start doubting all of your life choices, but keep at it – a little sunflower oil on your hands will work wonders. Dredge each ball in the melted chocolate, covering each by half. Transfer each one to a sheet of greaseproof paper to set before eating.

Toffee Apple and Salted Pretzel Rocky Road

While rocky road needs, obviously, to have a good crunch to it, it's important that we don't neglect chewiness and fruitiness. This is a triple threat. The wafers used here are those discs comprising two very thin biscuits, sandwiched together with an impossibly chewy layer of caramel – they're sometimes sold under their Dutch name: stroopwafel.

Makes 12–16
pieces

250g (9oz) dark chocolate (60–70% cocoa solids), broken into chunks
100g (3½oz) milk chocolate, broken into chunks
125g (4½oz) salted butter
1 tbsp golden syrup

50g (1¾oz) mini marshmallows
100g (3½oz) caramel/toffee wafers (stroopwafel), roughly chopped
100g (3½oz) hazelnuts, roughly chopped
100g (3½oz) salted pretzels, roughly crushed
100g (3½oz) dried apple, roughly chopped

Line a 20cm (8in) square cake tin with baking paper.

Put both the chocolates, butter and the golden syrup into a medium saucepan and set over a medium-low heat. Stirring frequently, allow everything to melt together into a smooth, chocolatey pool.

Put all the remaining ingredients into a large mixing bowl.

Pour the chocolate mixture into the mixing bowl and stir so that everything is evenly mixed and coated in the chocolate. Scoop into the prepared cake tin, press down to level and refrigerate for an hour or until set solid. Cut into the desired number and sized pieces.

Apricot, Whisky and Honey Cheesecake

I tend to shy away from deconstructed desserts. Being a classically trained pastry chef, I like structure and foundation and find it hard to veer away from that discipline. Whimsical platefuls can be intimidating: reserved only for the trendiest of restaurants, reviewed critically by an entire hipster team. In contrast to this, most food writers will have simplicity at the core of their professional integrity – if our recipes are too technical, they won't be used. But putting these probably too-profound reflections aside, this is simply a blob of a cream cheese mixture topped with some toasted oats and poached apricots. How can that be anything other than desirable?

Serves 4

For the apricots
6–8 small apricots,
   halved and stoned
300ml (10fl oz) water
150g (5oz) honey
   (chestnut honey is perfect)
75ml (2½fl oz) single malt whisky
3 cloves
3 cardamom pods
1 star anise

For the cheesecake
125ml (4¼fl oz) double cream
½ tsp vanilla extract
2 tbsp honey
150g (5oz) full-fat Greek yogurt
280g (10oz) full-fat cream cheese

For the base
75g (2¾oz) jumbo porridge oats
25g (1oz) butter
40g (1½oz) dark brown
   muscovado sugar

Start with the apricots. Place them in a medium saucepan along with the water, honey, whisky, cloves, cardamom pods and star anise. Bring to a simmer and cook gently for 20 minutes.

Meanwhile, put the cream into a mixing bowl with the vanilla and honey and whisk to very soft peaks. Throw in the yogurt and cream cheese and whisk until smooth.

Put a large deep-sided frying or sauté pan over a high heat. When the pan is hot, add the oats and toast, tossing occasionally, for a minute. Add the butter and sugar and fry, stirring, until the oats are caramelised – a couple of minutes. Remove from the heat and allow to cool.

To serve, scoop generously heaping mounds of the cream cheese mixture into four bowls. Add the poached apricot halves and sprinkle over the oats. Drizzle over a little of the warm poaching syrup and serve.

Pumpkin Spice Latte Rice Pudding

Much as I love a traditional rice pudding, with stout grains of rice flavoured only with nutmeg and jam, there's a lot to be said for this quicker, up-to-date version. The combination of flavours is something I'm sure most of you will be familiar with now – it has been a 'trend' for many years. And while I usually turn my nose up at food trends, this is one that I have fallen deeply in love with – not least because it's so inextricably linked to Christmas, my favourite holiday. This version uses basmati rice, which is much quicker to cook. It's important that you don't wash the rice as you normally would, as that extra starch will only serve to further thicken this bowl of gloopy joy.

Serves 4

150g (5oz) basmati rice
300ml (10fl oz) water
250ml (9fl oz) whole milk
50ml (2fl oz) double cream
100g (3½oz) canned pumpkin purée
   (I use Libby's)
100ml (3½fl oz) maple syrup
1 tsp ground ginger
1 tsp ground cinnamon
¼ tsp freshly grated nutmeg
Fine sea salt

For the cream top
200ml (7fl oz) double cream
25ml (1½ tbsp) maple syrup
1 tsp coffee extract

To decorate
Chocolate-covered
   coffee beans (optional)
25g (1oz) dark chocolate (60–70%
   cocoa solids), finely grated

Put the basmati rice, water and a pinch of salt into a medium saucepan with a lid. Bring the water to the boil, then reduce to a simmer and cover. Cook for 7–10 minutes, until the rice is fairly soft and the water has all evaporated. Do keep a watchful eye on the pan, and if it boils dry too quickly, just add a splash of water.

Stir the rice well, scraping it off the bottom of the pan, then add the milk, cream, pumpkin purée, maple syrup and spices, with a pinch each of salt and pepper. Bring to the boil, then reduce to a gentle simmer and cook, stirring frequently, for 10–15 minutes, until very thick and gloopy.

Meanwhile, make the cream top. Put the cream, maple syrup and coffee extract into a mixing bowl and whisk to very soft and floppy peaks – the cream should hold peaks that threaten to disappear if you so much as look at them wrong.

Divide the rice pudding among four bowls and dollop a generous mound of the coffee cream on top. Finish with a scattering of the coffee beans, if using, and a grating of dark chocolate.

Chocolate Olive Oil Mousse

The title and ingredient list here may cause a state of panic, but please rest assured that there are no errors: olive oil and mayonnaise are both key ingredients. The olive oil is mostly for flavour, because its peppery bite marries well with the chocolate. The mayonnaise is merely for texture – because it is an emulsion, it helps to bind the chocolate with the egg whites, giving you the silkiest chocolate mousse imaginable.

Makes 4

250g (9oz) dark chocolate (60–70% cocoa solids), roughly chopped
65g (2¼oz) organic mayonnaise
6 large egg whites

3 tbsp caster sugar
200g (7oz) full-fat crème fraîche
4 tsp extra virgin olive oil
Sea salt flakes, to serve

Have handy four champagne coupes or small jars.

Put the chocolate and mayonnaise into a heatproof bowl and set over a saucepan of barely simmering water. Stirring occasionally, allow the chocolate and mayonnaise to melt together.

Meanwhile, put the egg whites into a second bowl and whisk to stiff peaks. Add the sugar and whisk in until combined.

Once the chocolate is melted, remove from the heat and wipe the base of the bowl to prevent water splashing into the mousse. Take about a quarter of the egg whites and beat it into the chocolate, then scrape the chocolate mixture into the bowl with the remaining egg whites and gently fold together until fully incorporated and smooth. Divide the mousse among the glasses or jars. While this will be delicious to eat straight away, it's best once it has set for an hour or so in the fridge.

Just before serving, dollop the crème fraîche on top of the mousse and finish with a drizzle of olive oil and a sprinkle of sea salt.

Leftover egg yolks:

Yolks freeze beautifully. It's best to beat them with a pinch of salt to stop the protein thickening in the freezer, then just pop them into an airtight container, label them and store them in the freezer. You should use them within 6 months.

Banana and Pecan Steamed Puddings with Whisky Custard

As we grow, and our naïve and superficial hopes are eroded by reality, we learn to pay no mind to what other people may expect of us. When I started out my career as a food writer, I was under the impression that everything should be made from scratch and only the best ingredients should be used. I now believe that in food, convenience can sometimes (not always) outweigh preparing every element. This sentiment was ignited by my teacher at Le Cordon Bleu, in London, who made a trifle with Bird's custard powder. The pudding here is comfort in a bowl, and the whisky custard is temporarily life-enhancing.

Makes 4

1 ripe banana, peeled
125g (4½oz) salted butter,
   at room temperature
60g (2¼oz) light muscovado sugar
65g (2¼oz) caster sugar
2 large eggs
125g (4½oz) plain flour
2 tbsp cocoa powder
½ tsp baking powder
75g (2¾oz) white chocolate chips

75g (2¾oz) pecans, roughly chopped
½ tsp vanilla extract
Flavourless oil, for greasing
2 bananas, sliced and caramelised (optional)

For the whisky custard
500ml (18fl oz) whole milk
4 tbsp honey
3 tbsp whisky
75g (2¾oz) Bird's custard powder

Fill a large saucepan with hot water, set a steaming basket with a lid on top and bring to the boil.

Put the banana into a mixing bowl and mash with a fork. Add the butter, sugars, eggs, flour, powders, chocolate chips, pecans and vanilla extract and, with a hand-held electric mixer, beat to a smooth batter with lumps of banana and the chocolate chips and pecans.

Liberally grease four 175ml (6fl oz) pudding moulds with the oil and divide the batter among them. Cover each pudding mould with a flattened cupcake paper case, folding it over the edges of the pudding mould. Secure the paper cases onto the moulds with elastic bands. Steam the puddings for 25–30 minutes, until a skewer inserted into the centre comes out reasonably clean – there might be the odd blob of banana and chocolate, but don't mistake that for raw batter.

While the puddings steam, make the custard. Put all but 2 tablespoons of the milk into a saucepan with the honey and whisky and bring to a boil. Put the remaining milk and the custard powder into a small bowl and beat to a paste. Once the milk is boiling, pour it onto the custard powder mixture, then pour it all back into the pan and set over a medium-high heat. Stir constantly, until the custard has thickened. Remove from the heat.

Serve each pudding, warm, drowned in a sea of boozy custard and topped with banana slices, if using.

Apricot and Cardamom Upside-down Pudding

It may seem gratuitous to make an upside-down pudding in a frying pan, but this method is somewhat of a pleasant surprise. The direct heat means that the bottom (which will, when inverted, become the top) becomes deeply caramelised and chewy, then you add the lid and the rest of the cake steams and becomes dense like a pudding. I think this method would work with most fruits – I'm tempted to try strawberries with black cardamom and orange next.

For the caramel base
100g (3½oz) caster sugar
9-10 small apricots,
   halved and destoned

For the batter
170g (6oz) unsalted butter,
   at room temperature
170g (6oz) caster sugar
3 large eggs
170g (6oz) self-raising flour
½ tbsp ground cardamom

Crème fraîche, to serve

Serves 8–10

Set a medium deep-sided frying or sauté pan over a high heat. Once the pan is hot, add the sugar and allow it to melt into a rusty-coloured caramel. If the sugar starts to burn, just remove it from the heat and give it a gentle stir. Reduce the heat to medium-low and add the apricot halves, cut-side down. Allow the apricots to cook gently while you make the cake batter.

Put the butter and sugar into a mixing bowl and beat vigorously with a wooden spoon until pale in colour and fluffy in texture – if you have a hand-held electric mixer this would be the right time to root it out. Add the eggs, flour and ground cardamom, and beat to a smooth batter. Dollop the batter on top of the apricots, then spread out as best you can using the back of a spoon. The beauty of this pudding lies solely in the eating; it wouldn't win any awards for its good looks, so don't worry if it's a bit gnarly.

Cover the pan with a lid and cook over a low heat for 30–35 minutes, or until the cake batter is just set. Flip onto a large plate or cake stand and serve with dollops of crème fraîche.

Charcoal and Guinness Dampfnudel with Blackberry and Cassis Compote

I'm torn. Do I first address what the hell this dish is, or do I talk about using charcoal? Well, dampfnudel, usually plain white, is a steamed bun most popular in southern Germany. Ordinarily they are made using a yeasted dough, be we don't have time for that in this book, so I make these with baking powder and Guinness instead. The Guinness is, of course, there for its ferric, malty flavour, but its bubbles also help to aerate the dough wonderfully. The charcoal is there merely for colour – yes, I'm that shallow when it comes to my dishes. I wanted these buns to be deeply black so that the equally dark compote both glazes and complements them. Charcoal powder is readily available online, but if it doesn't float your dampfnudel, leave it out.

Makes 6

For the dampfnudel
250g (9oz) plain flour
10g (⅓oz) activated charcoal powder
25g (1oz) unsalted butter
40g (1½oz) caster sugar
10g (⅓oz) baking powder
75ml (2½fl oz) Guinness
1 large egg

For the poaching liquid
100ml (3½fl oz) whole milk
15g (½oz) butter
15g (½oz) sugar

For the blackberry and cassis compote
600g (¼lb) blackberries
200g (7oz) caster sugar
2 tbsp crème de cassis

Double cream, whipped, to serve

First make the dough for the dampfnudel. Put the flour, charcoal powder and butter into a mixing bowl and rub together to fine breadcrumbs. Add the remaining ingredients and stir into a smooth dough. Once the dough is too stiff to stir with a spoon, get your hands in there and knead briefly until smooth. Divide the dough into six even portions, rolling each into a neat ball.

Put the ingredients for the poaching liquid into a large, flameproof casserole and set over a high heat. Once the milk starts to boil, reduce the heat to low, drop in the balls of dough, giving them space to expand, and cover with a lid. Steam for 20 minutes, then remove the lid and continue cooking until the liquid has almost entirely evaporated (it may already have done so). The bases of the dampfnudel should be slightly caramelised and charred.

Meanwhile, put the blackberries and sugar into a small saucepan, add a tablespoon of water, and bring to the boil. Cook until the blackberries are more or less broken down, then remove from the heat and stir in the crème de cassis. Serve the dampfnudel in bowls and spoon over the blackberry and cassis compote. Serve with a blob of whipped cream.

Plum, Earl Grey and Star Anise Cobbler

Cobblers beat crumble. I know this will be a polarising statement but look at it from this angle: with a cobbler you get the fruit with what is pretty much a soft, steamed scone on top. What's more, crumbles, when made by the wrong fingers, are often too dry and coat your teeth with that horrible fizz of baking powder and undercooked flour. No, I make no bones about my preference here, and hope this recipe will convince you likewise.

1 Earl Grey tea bag	**For the cobbles**
125ml (4fl oz) boiling water	125g (4½oz) self-raising wholemeal flour
30g (1oz) unsalted butter	25g (1oz) unsalted butter
2 star anise	Zest of 1 unwaxed orange
125g (4½oz) light brown muscovado sugar	1 tbsp caster sugar
	1 tsp baking powder
700g (1½lb) large plums, quartered and stoned	1 tbsp milk
	1 large egg
Juice of 1 orange	
300g (10½oz) crème fraîche, to serve	

Serves 4

First make the Earl Grey tea. Put the tea bag into a mug and pour over the boiling water. Leave to infuse for 3 minutes.

Set a medium, deep-sided frying or sauté pan over a high heat and add the butter, star anise and sugar. Allow the butter to melt and combine with the sugar to create a slick of butterscotch, then add the plums, orange juice and tea. Reduce the heat to medium-high and cook the plums for 5 minutes.

Meanwhile, make the cobbles. Put the flour into a mixing bowl and rub in the butter until you have fine breadcrumbs. Toss through the orange zest, sugar and baking powder, then add the milk and egg. Mix to a fairly stiff dough, using your hands or a wooden spoon. Rip off ping-pong ball-sized pieces and pop them on top of the plums. Reduce the heat to medium-low, cover the pan with a lid and steam for 15–20 minutes. The cobbles should swell up and sink slightly below the pool of fruit. Serve immediately with blobs of cold crème fraîche.

Passion Fruit Tiramisu

In deference to its name, any tiramisu I make must always contain coffee. The Italian Tira *(pull)* mi *(me)* su *(on) loosely translates to 'pick me up', so unless it's spiked with one of those godawful caffeine drinks, it must have the coffee. But that isn't to say it need be coffee alone. Many flavours are well suited to the bitter tang of coffee – perhaps surprisingly, passion fruit is one of the best.*

Makes 4

8 ladyfinger sponges

3 tbsp Kahlúa liqueur

1 tbsp instant coffee granules

4 passion fruit

500g (18oz) mascarpone

100g (3½oz) passion fruit yogurt

75ml condensed milk

Break up the ladyfingers and divide them evenly among four wine glasses. In a small bowl, mix together the Kahlúa, instant coffee, 3 tablespoons of water and the pulp of 3 of the passion fruit. Divide this mixture among the wine glasses, pressing down the sponges to soak them well.

For the cream, put the mascarpone, yogurt and condensed milk into a mixing bowl and whisk until smooth. Divide the cream among the wine glasses, carefully spooning it on top of the soaked sponges. Refrigerate for 20 minutes.

Just before serving, top with the pulp from the remaining passion fruit.

season the day

An organised mind

While writing this book, I took a break and headed for Canada. It was New Year's Day and I realised that life had just gotten too heavy. At times, even the mundanities of everyday life are mountainous, and for me I'm afraid, it was a case of do or die. I had to escape my life, take stock and recover.

I decided to volunteer on a farm in British Columbia. Friends had told me of the Wwoof programme (I think it stands for World Wide Opportunities on Organic Farms) and how healing it can be. I joined the website, found a host family who needed help urgently – a husband and wife who owned a small farm which they tended solely for the purpose of survival – and packed my bags.

Life on the farm was exactly that: living. There was no mobile phone signal to tempt my fingers, no television to convey sadness or tragedy. I wasn't plagued by #FakeNews or knee-jerk reactions to something a celebrity may or may not have said. I replaced Twitter for real birdsong. That made me realise that social media, once a vibrant hub of birdsong, can sometimes be a vast echoing canyon with only vultures circling the rim.

The most virtuous part of the whole experience, though, was the sense of recalibration. When you work for yourself, it is easy to drift off into bad routines: working all night, sleeping all day. I had lost the fizz and excitement of my career and became careless and sloppy. Working with animals, however, changed that. Every morning I was solely responsible for the food, water and welfare of the beasts – dogs, chickens, pigs, sheep and cows. As I plucked the eggs from beneath warm, broody hens, and shattered thick ice on top of the cows' water trough so they could drink, I rediscovered gratitude.

At night, I would repeat the animal husbandry and I found myself becoming the organised creature I once was. I'd get their buckets of water and food ready for the morning. I drew parallels with that and this book project, thinking: if we can care for these animals with such dignity and respect, we should do the same for ourselves. I find that preparing dinner in the morning fills us with a sense of virtuous organisation – one that echoes through the caverns of everyday life. The recipes in this chapter are therefore quick to throw together in the morning, and just as quick to finish off when you return home at night. With a little morning prep, you can achieve lightening evening speed.

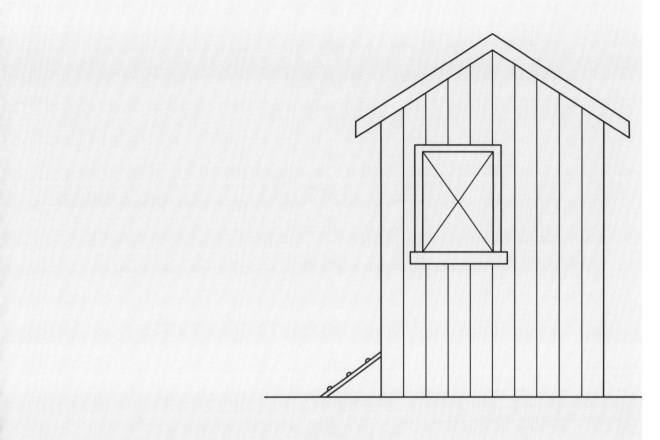
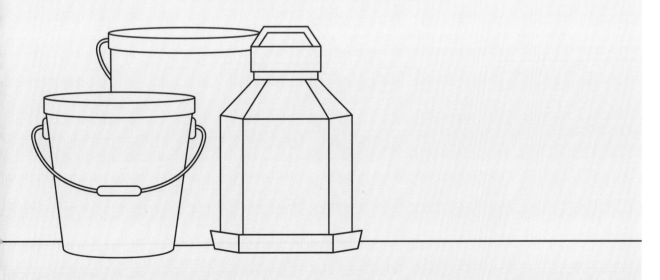

Jalapeño Chicken Burgers
with Cheddar Corn Fritters

The relationship between brine and pickle is entirely bilateral. While the assumption is that the brine imparts its salty acidity into whatever it is protecting, it's also prudent to remember that the product imparts some flavour into the brine. To chuck that down the sink would be a travesty. The brine here gives the chicken a subtle spice – though it won't blow your head off. I fry the corn fritters encircled by pepper rings – not only does this maintain their shape, but I find them to be the perfect size to slide onto a brioche bun.

Serves 4

500g (18oz) chicken mini fillets
215g (7½oz) jar sliced green jalapeños
1 tbsp olive oil

For the Fritters
1 large egg
50g (1¾oz) plain flour
198g (7oz) can sweetcorn (keep the juice)
50g (1¾oz) mature Cheddar, grated
2 tbsp finely chopped chives,
    plus extra for sprinkling

2 spring onions, finely chopped
1 tbsp olive oil
1 large red pepper, sliced into 6 thick rings
Fine sea salt and freshly ground black pepper

To serve
4 brioche buns, sliced
Mayonnaise, for spreading
Handful of baby spinach leaves
Tabasco sauce
Chips, to serve (optional)

Put the chicken into a mixing bowl and pour over the liquid from the jar of chillies (leave the chillies in the jar, remove 1 tablespoon, chop and reserve) as well as the juice from the can of sweetcorn (decant the sweetcorn into a small bowl and pop into the fridge). Cover the bowl and refrigerate for 8 hours.

When you're ready to cook, drain and discard the marinade from the chicken. Preheat a large frying pan over a medium-high heat and add the olive oil. Once the oil is hot, add the chicken and fry for 4–5 minutes per side, until lightly golden and cooked through. Transfer the chicken to a plate and cover with foil or another plate to keep warm.

Meanwhile, make the fritter batter. Put the egg into a mixing bowl and add 2 tablespoons water. Whisk to combine, then whisk in the flour to a thick paste. Switch to a wooden spoon and fold through the sweetcorn, cheese, chives, spring onions, chopped jalapeños and a generous pinch of salt and pepper.

When the chicken is cooked, wipe the pan with kitchen paper, then return to the heat and add the olive oil. Add the pepper rings and fill each one with batter, overfilling them slightly. Fry for 3 minutes, flip, and fry for a further 3 minutes. The fritters should be darkly coloured and set. To assemble, spread the buns with mayo, then stack them high with fritters, chicken, spinach and Tabasco – and don't forget to sprinkle over some of those leftover jalapeños. Serve with chips on the side, if using.

Saffron Za'atar and Lemon Chicken Kebabs

What I love most about this recipe is that the marinade is both effective in its tenderising qualities, and entirely visual. As you mix together the yogurt and saffron it will be a little disappointing – the only golden hues will be small flecks within the yogurt. But after a day in the fridge, the yogurt will be marbled with rich yellow smears, both regal and warming in tone. The za'atar in this recipe was an afterthought, one that my dear friend Stacy, who tested this for me all the way over in New York, recommended. I'm entirely grateful, and so, Stacy, this recipe is dedicated to you.

Serves 4

For the chicken

500g (18oz) chicken mini fillets

5 tbsp full-fat Greek yogurt

Generous pinch of saffron strands

Zest of 1 unwaxed lemon

½ tsp chilli powder

To finish

2 tbsp olive oil

1 red onion, sliced into fine rings

1 yellow pepper, deseeded and sliced into fine rings

1 lemon (from the marinade)

4 flatbread wraps

4 tbsp hummus

2 tsp za'atar spice

Sea salt flakes and freshly ground black pepper

In the morning, put the chicken into a bowl with the yogurt, saffron, lemon zest, chilli powder and a few twists of black pepper. Stir to coat everything well, cover the bowl with a plate and pop into the fridge. Leave the house with smug reassurance that dinner is prepared.

When you're ready to cook, heat the oil in a frying pan over a medium-high heat. Once the oil shimmers and moves freely around the pan, add the chicken. Try to cover the chicken well with the marinade as you remove each piece from the bowl. Fry the chicken on each side for 3–5 minutes, or until slightly charred but the sunny yellow still gleams through the blackened cage and the chicken is cooked through – I always cut the fattest fillet in half to ensure everything is cooked. Put the chicken onto a plate, wipe the oil from the pan with a piece of kitchen paper and return the pan to a high heat.

Fry the onion and peppers in the wiped pan, just for a few minutes until coloured but not softened. Quarter the lemon and add it to the pan, frying on each cut side for a minute or so, until charred. Pop the lemon, onion and peppers on the plate with the chicken.

Place the flatbreads, one at a time, into the hot pan and fry for just a few seconds per side to heat through. Spread hummus onto each flatbread and top with the chicken, peppers and onion. Sprinkle over the za'atar, season with salt and a little more pepper, and serve with juice from the charred lemon. Behold the ravishing colours, then wrap it up and snaffle.

Pork Gyros

Throughout Greece, and many Mediterranean countries, gyros are a firm favourite for tourists and natives alike. They are simply meat kebabs, and their name comes from the vertical spit on which the meat would traditionally be cooked. While I'm not able (but, strangely, so willing) to install a vertical spit in my kitchen, that shouldn't be a reason not to make something as delicious as this. It's also a great way of making one piece of meat go a long way.

For the pork	For the kebabs	Serves 2
1 pork loin steak, fat removed	2 tbsp olive oil	
1 tbsp full-fat Greek yogurt	2 Mediterranean-style flatbreads	
½ tsp dried thyme	2 heaped tbsp tzatziki	
½ tsp dried oregano	1 tomato, roughly diced	
½ tsp celery salt	½ small red onion, finely sliced	
½ tsp black pepper	¼ cucumber, peeled and sliced	
	50g (1¾oz) feta cheese	
	A few drops of cider vinegar	
	Fine sea salt	

In the morning, put the pork steak into a mixing bowl and add the remaining pork ingredients. Rub everything into the meat to create a marinade. Cover the bowl and refrigerate until it's time to cook.

When you're ready to cook, heat a large, deep-sided frying or sauté pan over a high heat and add the oil. Once the oil shimmers, reduce the heat to medium-high and add the pork. Fry for 3 minutes per side – but do slice into it in the middle to check it's cooked all the way through – then pop onto a plate to rest for a few minutes.

Wipe out the pan and return it to a high heat. Warm the flatbreads for 15 seconds or so per side.

To assemble, spread tzatziki onto each flatbread. Top with the tomato, onion and cucumber. Thinly slice the pork and add it to the kebab, then crumble over the feta, drizzle over a little vinegar and season with salt.

Make it even better: if you fancy, and have the time, pop to the local chippy and get a portion of chips. Put a small handful into each wrap.

Hot Dog Bahn Mí

When disparate cultures collide, delicious things can happen. Hot dogs, it is rumoured, were first sold in New York in the nineteenth century by German immigrants. During the protectorate of French Indochina around that same time, baguettes became popular in Vietnam – it was a big century for the little bread roll. I wanted to further entangle things to create this, the Hot Dog Bahn Mí. Bahn Mí, for those who have never been lucky enough to encounter its deliciousness, is a baguette filled with pâté, flavoured meats and pickled vegetables. Stick a sausage in that and you've got something that would be most welcome on my last-meal buffet table.

Makes 4

For the pickles

2 pickled cucumbers from a jar,
   finely sliced
4 tbsp liquid from the jar
   of cucumbers
4 radishes, finely sliced
1 carrot, coarsely grated
1 small red onion, finely sliced
2 tbsp rice wine vinegar

To assemble

4 jumbo Frankfurter sausages
4 individual-sized baguettes,
   split down the middle
4 tbsp smooth pâté
4 tbsp mayonnaise of choice
   (I like the Kewpie brand)
1 tbsp dark soy sauce
Small handful of coriander*,
   roughly chopped

In the morning, put the sliced cucumbers into a bowl with the pickle liquid, radishes, carrot, onion and rice wine vinegar. Cover and set to one side until needed, either lunchtime or the evening.

When you're ready to cook the hot dogs, set the griddle pan over a medium–high heat. Once the pan is hot, add the Frankfurters (it's probably wise to stab them a couple of times before to avoid an almighty, all-meaty, explosion). Fry, turning once, for 5 minutes or so – just until they are hot, and the griddle pan has branded them with black bar marks.

Meanwhile, spread each baguette with pâté (I do both sides). When the sausages are cooked, put one into each baguette along with the pickled bits and bobs – you'd think there'd be far too many pickles to fit into the sandwiches, but cram them in like commuters on the London underground. Drizzle the mayo and soy over the filling. Finish with a scattering of coriander and serve.

* If you can find coriander cress, use that instead.

Sriracha and Pomegranate Lamb with Beetroot Tabbouleh

It's often the weird and wonderful, utterly disparate ingredients that unify to make the most satisfying of meals. Pomegranate molasses, with its lip-puckering tanginess, marries very well with the salty spice of sriracha chilli sauce. The tabbouleh is earthy, but offers random bursts of revitalising sweetness as the pomegranate seeds pop in the mouth.

Serves 4

For the lamb
8 lamb cutlets
1 tbsp olive oil
4 tbsp sriracha
2 tbsp pomegranate molasses
1 tsp fine sea salt
30g (1oz) unsalted butter

For the tabbouleh
250g (9oz) cracked bulgar wheat
600ml (1 pint) boiling water
2 large handfuls of flat-leaf
    parsley, finely chopped
3 small beetroot, peeled and
    coarsely grated
4 spring onions, finely sliced
Seeds from 1 pomegranate
Extra virgin olive oil
Sea salt flakes and coarse
    black pepper

In the morning, put the lamb into a mixing bowl and add the other ingredients except the butter. Stir together until the lamb is evenly coated – I find it easiest (not to mention incredibly satisfying) to use my hands. Cover the bowl and refrigerate all day.

When you're ready to cook, put the bulgar wheat into another mixing bowl and cover with the boiling water. Cover and leave to soak for 15–20 minutes while you cook the lamb.

Heat a large frying pan over a high heat. Once the pan is very hot, add the lamb cutlets and fry for 2½ minutes per side. In the last 30 seconds throw in the butter and allow it to fizz and foam, using a spoon to baste the lamb with it. Once cooked, put the lamb on a plate to rest, and pour over the cooked butter.

Once the bulgar wheat is soft, drain away any excess water, then add the parsley, beetroot, spring onions, pomegranate seeds, a very generous drizzle of extra virgin olive oil and salt and pepper to taste. Serve an enticing mound of tabbouleh topped with the tender lamb cutlets.

51

Pickle Philly Steak Nachos

Whenever I buy a jar of pickles, I am loath to pour away that precious liquor. It seems disrespectful to discard something that has imparted so much flavour, and has offered months of protection. This is the perfect use for that juice. And while this recipe requires both brine and cornichons, in the future you can save the juice and use it to marinate meat.

Serves 4

2 x 225g (8oz) sirloin steaks
170g (6oz) jar cornichons
1 tbsp sunflower oil
1 green pepper, deseeded and finely diced
1 onion, finely sliced
200g (7oz) tortilla chips
1 tbsp jalapeños, from a jar
Sea salt flakes and freshly ground black pepper
Fresh limes, to serve

For the cheese sauce
30g (1oz) unsalted butter
30g (1oz) plain flour
250ml (9fl oz) milk
150g (5oz) Red Leicester, grated

In the morning, remove the fat from the steaks and put them into a mixing bowl. Pour the liquid from the jar of cornichons onto the steak. Cover and refrigerate for the day.

When you're ready to cook, remove the steak from the fridge and drain away the liquid. Finely slice the steak into thin, floppy rags, and season the steak generously with salt.

For the cheese sauce, set a medium saucepan over a high heat. Once the pan is hot, add the butter and allow it to melt, then add the flour and quickly beat to a smooth paste with a wooden spoon. Add the milk slowly, beating constantly – the mixture will thicken as the first few drops of milk are added, but keep going until you have a smooth sauce. Reduce the heat to low, stir in the cheese until melted and season to taste. Leave to thicken while you fry everything else – remember to stir the pan every so often.

Put the oil into a large, deep-sided frying or sauté pan over a high heat. When the oil is hot, add the steak and fry until lightly charred and cooked through. Remove from the pan and set onto a plate. Return the pan to a high heat and add the pepper and onion. Fry, tossing the pan, until the peppers are charred and the onion is a little softer and lightly coloured – a few minutes.

To assemble, put the tortilla chips on a large serving plate. Scatter over the steak and the fried onions and peppers. Roughly chop the cornichons (maybe not all of them) and scatter along with the jalapeños. Pour over the cheese sauce and sprinkle with salt and pepper. Add a squeeze of fresh lime juice just before serving.

Beef Bulgogi with Sushi Rice

Bulgogi is a Korean dish of marinated meat – usually beef. Its name translates to fire meat and it would normally be cooked on a barbecue, but like many modern Korean families and cooks, I do mine in a frying pan. The key is to let the beef marinate for the day, and while kiwi seems an odd ingredient here – indeed it is – I use it as a substitute for Asian pear, which is more difficult to come by in the UK. Both form an enzymatic marinade, which tenderises the meat beyond belief. Another diversion from authenticity is my use of gochujang – Korean spicy soy bean paste. While it is completely optional, I love the added fieriness it injects into the dish. If you like fire but can't find the paste, just throw a chopped chilli or two into the marinade.

Serves 4

For the beef
2 x 225g (8oz) sirloin steaks,
   finely sliced
4 tbsp light soy sauce
2 tsp caster sugar
2 garlic cloves, minced
2 spring onions, finely chopped
½ kiwi fruit, peeled and finely chopped
1 tbsp gochujang paste (optional)

1 tbsp sesame oil
250g (9oz) sushi rice
2 tbsp sunflower oil, for frying
1 onion, sliced

To garnish
1 tbsp sesame seeds
2 spring onions, finely sliced

Put the sliced sirloin into a mixing bowl and add the soy, sugar, garlic, spring onions, kiwi fruit, gochujang, if using, and sesame oil. Cover the bowl and refrigerate for the day.

When you are ready to cook, take the bowl from the fridge. Put the sushi rice into a sieve and wash under cold water for a good minute until the water runs clear. Put the rice in a medium saucepan with 330ml (11fl oz) water and bring to a boil. Reduce to a simmer and cook for 9 minutes, then put a lid on the pan, remove from the heat and leave the pot to stand for 25 minutes. Don't even dare to peek inside the pan, just let it stand and steam.

When the rice is just about ready, heat a large, deep-sided frying or sauté pan over a high heat. When the pan is hot, add the sunflower oil and allow it to get so hot that it shimmers. Add the onion and stir-fry for a few minutes until it softens and colours. Add the beef and fry for a couple of minutes per side. It's likely that the beef will release lots of liquid, so stirring the pan will make the beef braise. If you leave it alone until the liquid has reduced, the beef should start to colour. When it does, give it a stir or a toss, and cook to the desired stage – I like it medium rare.

Serve mounds of sticky sushi rice, topped with tender rags of bulgogi beef. Finish with a scattering of sesame seeds and some sliced spring onions.

Marinated Hanger Steak with Creamed Corn

This steakhouse pairing is a classic, and one that I have enjoyed in many different places, in many different permutations. I think this version is up there with my favourites, not least because hanger steak, I feel, could give even the finest fillet a run for its money. The creamed corn is a twist on the Mexican street food of grilled corn, known as elotes. I've used the same combination of spices, cheese and soured cream here as a nod to it.

Hanger steak – also known as the 'butcher's steak', which alludes to its desirable succulence and flavour – often comes in one large slab when bought at the butcher's. Some supermarkets do fillet the steaks, and it's the individually sized portion that this recipe calls for.

Serves 2

For the steak
Juice of 2 limes
2 tbsp light soy sauce
2 tbsp Worcestershire sauce
1 onion, finely chopped
2 small hanger steaks
1 tbsp sunflower oil
Sea salt flakes

For the creamed corn
200ml (7fl oz) double cream
2 garlic cloves, crushed
½ tsp ground cumin
½ tsp paprika
2 corn cobs
45g (1⅔oz) Parmesan, finely grated
50g (1¾oz) soured cream
Small handful of parsley, roughly chopped
1 spring onion, finely sliced
Freshly ground black pepper

If you have the willpower to wake up 5 minutes earlier than normal, get started on marinating the steak in the morning. Put the lime juice, soy and Worcestershire sauce into a mixing bowl with the chopped onion and 1 teaspoon of sea salt flakes. Add the steaks, coat well with the marinade, then cover and refrigerate for the day.

When you're ready to cook everything, get the steaks out of the fridge and let them come to room temperature.

For the creamed corn, put the cream, garlic, cumin and paprika into a medium saucepan and bring to the boil. As soon as it boils, remove the pan from the heat and allow to infuse while you continue with everything else.

Set a large frying pan over a high heat. Once the pan is hot, add the sunflower oil and allow that to get very hot. Add the hanger steaks to the pan (leaving the marinade in the bowl),

reduce the heat to medium-high and fry the steaks for 4–5 minutes per side. Remove the steaks from the pan and wrap in foil to rest and stay warm.

While the steaks rest, remove the corn kernels from the cob: stand a cob upright, then run a sharp knife down the cob, shaving off the kernels. I love how the knife rattles and judders as it glides through the humps of corn. Repeat with the other cob, and add the kernels to the pan with the cream. Return the saucepan to a high heat and allow the cream to come to a boil once more. Remove from the heat and stir in the Parmesan and soured cream. Season well with salt and pepper.

Divide the creamed corn between two shallow serving bowls or plates. Slice the hanger steak, ensuring you slice it against the grain to achieve maximum tenderness, and lay the slices on top of the creamed corn. Drizzle over the resting juices from the plate, and finish with a sprinkling of chopped parsley and sliced spring onion.

Monkfish and Anise Stew

I wouldn't dare call this dish a bouillabaisse – I'd fear the wrath of all of Marseille if I were to try to draw even the faintest of comparisons; though the flavour combination – fish and anise (whether from dill, fennel, Pernod or pastis) – really is inspired by bouillabaisse. Although I've called this a stew, it's really more of a broth: light and delicate. The colour is a deep purple, somewhat reminiscent of a Ukrainian borscht, thanks to the purple carrot, although an orange one would work, too.

For the monkfish
600g (1¼lb) monkfish fillets,
   cut into large chunks
2 tbsp sea salt flakes
1 tsp caster sugar
Zest of 1 unwaxed orange
2 star anise

For the stew
2 tbsp olive oil
1 large onion, finely sliced
1 celery stick, finely sliced

1 purple carrot, finely sliced
   (orange is fine if you can't get purple)
2 garlic cloves, finely sliced
1 star anise
1 tomato, roughly chopped
125ml (4fl oz) extra dry vermouth (or dry white wine)
400ml (14fl oz) chicken stock
Handful of dill, freshly chopped
Handful of parsley, freshly chopped
Juice of ½ lemon
Sea salt flakes and coarsely ground black pepper

Baguette and butter, to serve

Serves 4

In the morning, put the monkfish into a bowl and add the salt, sugar and orange zest. Roughly chop the star anise as best you can – this is a little grating, like the jolting feeling you might get if you imagine biting onto a nail file, but just grit your teeth and get it roughly chopped. Add the star anise to the bowl and toss everything together, coating the monkfish well. Cover the bowl with cling film or a plate and refrigerate until you are ready to start cooking.

Just before you start cooking, rinse the monkfish briefly under cold water. Pat dry with a clean tea towel. Don't worry about getting every chunk clean, just rinse off most of the cure ingredients.

In a large saucepan or deep-sided frying pan, heat the oil over a high heat. Once the oil starts to shimmer, add the onion, celery and carrot and fry on high, stirring very frequently, for 5 minutes. Add the garlic, anise and tomato and fry for another minute or so, then add the vermouth or wine and cook until it evaporates. Add the stock and bring to the boil, then reduce to a gentle simmer. Cook for 10 minutes, then stir in the dill, parsley and monkfish, and cook for a further 5 minutes or so, just until the monkfish is cooked but tender. Season to taste (you won't need much salt because of that cure), add the lemon juice and serve with torn chunks of buttered baguette.

table for one

straight from
the pan

Straight from the Pan

For millions of years food has been at the centre of community. It has been the glue that bonds social groups together, if not the very source from which such groups were born. Before the advent of agriculture, hunter-gatherers worked in cohorts, crossing their habitats in search of quarry, then sharing their spoils with their tribes.

While that primitive model may, in most developed countries, be long forgotten, its fervour still exists today. You need only to envisage a throbbing village fete or WI bake off to see the febrile effects that food can inflict upon a community. I often find myself giggling at such events, as I imagine those attending to be modern-day warriors, glamourised by gingham yet utterly political. And while that scenario is a far cry from the necessity of hunting for food, it's still an example of food as a highly social topic.

That notion of food is perpetuated by social media, with images of artisan, crafted wooden tables strewn with mismatched cutlery and crockery, surrounded by hordes of straight-toothed, flawless folk. These images group together to form the perfect template of a lifestyle aura that does, admittedly, have a certain pull. But does that template really reflect reality?

It isn't just social media that promotes that version of food. To a large extent the food-writing and broadcasting industries have exploited the idea of a crowded table. I myself am a culprit of that. I'm not shunning it; for the most part we do still eat together, and those feasts are something I personally revel in. But it's not unreasonable to surmise that, based on the emphasis on eating together and the severe lack of solo eating in the mainstream media, we perhaps view eating alone as a fairly sad state of affairs. We must not.

For a start, it isn't always practical to cook a recipe that would easily feed a family of six when there's just me, myself and I around the table. While I'm an advocate of batch-and-freeze cookery, that's not always achievable either. Sometimes we need to just rustle up a small something that we can slurp straight from the pan. It's recalibrating, at times, to flagrantly rebuff the notions of etiquette and just unclench.

Practicalities aside, I think cooking for just oneself should be celebrated. It is within those intimate moments that we find out more about ourselves – our likes, our tastes, our weaknesses and our flaws. This is a task that for many of us is life-long, and one that is sadly often never realised. What we choose to eat when alone reflects how we care for ourselves. Granted, a quick butty from the deli may be the only reasonable opportunity to eat, but when we have the time and facility to cook for ourselves, maybe we should embark on exactly that mission. I'm loath to employ the mass-marketed, narcissistic hyperbole of #SelfCare – which presents an equally unrealistic aura of a certain lifestyle – but the essence of that idea is such an important one: we need to love ourselves more than we currently do. Food is one of the best conveyors of love. As Audre Lorde wrote: 'Caring for myself is not self-indulgence, it is self-preservation'.

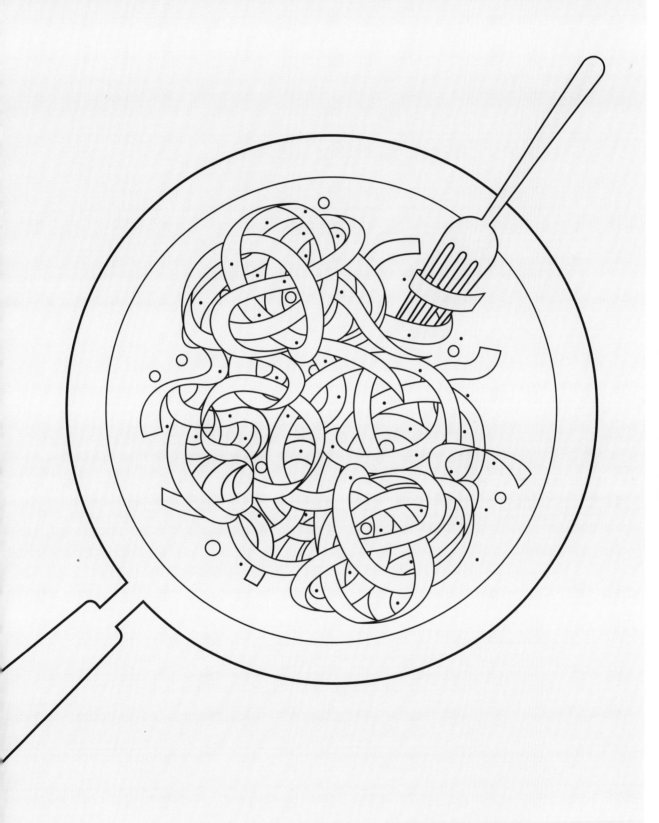

Chorizo and Membrillo
Grilled Cheese French Toast

Before we begin, let's get one thing straight: a grilled cheese sandwich is not just a cheese toasty.
A toasty is made in one of those pillow-shaped machines (preferably with a baked bean and Cheddar
filling). A grilled cheese sandwich, on the other hand, is fried in a golden pool of butter until ever
so crispy on the outside and oozing in the middle. This version is even better than either: the bread
is first treated like French toast, as it's dipped into an enriching pool of egg and milk. I've used
sourdough here, not because I'm a bread snob (I like my thick-cut white loaf as much as the next
person), but because it's firmer and so holds together when dunked. It's worth noting here, too, that
the chorizo in this recipe is the deli-style, ready-sliced stuff, and strictly not the cured loop kind.

Serves 1

1 large egg

2 tbsp whole milk

2 slices of sourdough bread

1 tsp membrillo or quince paste

8 slices of deli-style chorizo

40g (1½oz) aged Iberico cheese,
coarsely grated

40g (1½oz) ready-grated mozzarella

Unsalted butter, for frying

Beat the egg with the milk in a deep-rimmed plate. Dunk the sourdough into the egg mixture and allow it to soak for 30 seconds before flipping and repeating on the other side. Remove the bread and put it on a chopping board.

Onto one slice of bread, spread the membrillo or quince paste (it helps to beat it a bit before spreading) then top that with the chorizo slices. Pile the cheese on top of the meat (it will seem like an awful lot of cheese, but don't forget that it melts down to practically nothing!). Put the other slice of dunked bread on top.

Heat a generous knob of butter in a large, deep-sided frying or sauté pan set over a medium or medium-high heat. When the butter has melted and is hot, add the sandwich. I find it helps to place a piece of baking paper over the sandwich and a large heavy pan on top to heat it from both sides. Fry for 2–3 minutes until a very deep golden brown, then flip and repeat.

Japanese Pancake (Okonomiyaki)

This savoury pancake is up there with my favourite meals. A Japanese friend of mine once made their own version of Okonomiyaki (which translates to 'what you fancy, grilled') and I couldn't think about anything else for a good week afterwards. The vegetable flavour of the pancake is enhanced by the sweetness of the sauce and the tangy mayonnaise. (On that note, I like to use Kewpie mayonnaise, which is a little more acidic than the stuff we find here in the UK.) Normally the pancake is topped with a special okonomiyaki sauce, but if you live in even the most cosmopolitan area, it's not going to be something you'll stumble upon in the street, although mixing together a few storecupboard ingredients will offer a decent enough substitute. The pancakes are usually topped with dried seaweed and bonito flakes – if you come across these regularly, do grab them and add them at the end.

1 large egg

55g (2oz) plain flour

1 new potato, finely grated

2 spring onions, very finely sliced

125g (4½oz) Brussels sprouts, finely shredded

4 unsmoked streaky bacon rashers

Fine sea salt

To top

2 tbsp ketchup

2 tsp dark soy sauce

2 tsp Worcestershire sauce

2 tbsp mayonnaise
  (use the Kewpie brand, if possible)

Serves 1

First make the pancake batter. Simply whisk the egg and flour together in a mixing bowl into a very thick paste, then add 50ml (2fl oz) water and whisk to a smooth batter – if you whisk it well when it is thick, it's easier to avoid lumps. Add the potato, spring onions, sprouts and a generous pinch of salt – it will seem as though the batter is being overwhelmed by the vegetables, but that's precisely how it should be. Mix everything together as evenly as possible.

Heat a deep-sided frying pan with a lid over a medium heat and once the pan is hot, add the bacon rashers. Evenly pour all of the pancake batter over the rashers and press it down as neatly as possible using a wooden spoon or spatula – it doesn't matter if the batter doesn't completely fill the pan, as long as it covers the bacon and forms one compact disc rather than individual blobs, it'll be fine. Put a lid on the frying pan and fry for 5 minutes on one side, then flip and fry for a further 5 minutes on the other side.

While the pancake cooks, mix together the ketchup, soy and Worcestershire sauce in a small bowl.

When the pancake is ready, drizzle over the ketchup mixture and mayonnaise.

Lancashire e Pepe

It's always a risky business messing with Italian recipes; I find any deviations aren't taken lightly. I understand the need to maintain tradition and heritage, of course I do, but I don't believe small glimmers of personality should be smothered. And besides, I'm not sure that the dishes that receive such vehement protection are exact replicas of the first version ever made; if the original creator wishes to reincarnate herself and slap me about my kitchen, I will happily submit, but the pompous perpetuators will have to accept small twists.

This dish is my Lancashire version of the Roman classic, Cacio e Pepe *(pasta with cheese and black pepper), swapping out the traditionally used pecorino in favour of a cheese from my local ancestry – Lancashire.*

Serves 1

125g (4½oz) dried pappardelle
2 tsp freshly ground black pepper
(I like Tellicherry)

50g (1¾oz) Lancashire cheese,
coarsley grated
Sea salt flakes

Bring a medium saucepan of well-salted water to the boil and add the pasta. Boil for 1 minute less than stated on the packet instructions. Once the pasta is cooked, reserve 3 tablespoons of the cooking water (maybe a drop more), then drain the pasta.

Return the pan to the heat and add the pepper, frying it for just a second, then throw in the pasta and the reserved cooking water and swirl the pan, briefly, over the heat. Remove the pan from the heat and throw in the cheese. Stir vigorously until the cheese melts into the water to create a silky sauce. Season with salt, as required, and serve – though I like to eat this straight out of the pan.

Steak with Pak Choi and Ginger Chimichurri

Some friends once told me about their love for fried pak choi and chimichurri sauce, so I had to go a step further. Steak with chimichurri is necessary, but the pak choi is what inspired me to add the ginger and soy. The results are truly delicious. There will be leftover chimichurri, but just store it in a sealed jar in the fridge for up to a week.

1 sirloin steak	**For the chimichurri**	Serves 1
Olive oil	Small handful of parsley, finely chopped	
30g (1oz) unsalted butter	Small handful of coriander, finely chopped	
2 small pak choi, halved	1 tsp dried oregano	
Fine sea salt	1 red chilli, finely chopped	
	40g (1½oz) fresh ginger, peeled and grated	
	2 garlic cloves, grated	
	5 tbsp extra virgin olive oil	
	2 tbsp red wine vinegar	
	1 tbsp dark soy sauce	

To make the chimichurri, put the parsley and coriander into a bowl with the oregano. Add the chilli, ginger and garlic, then pour in the oil, vinegar and soy, and stir to combine. Taste and add fine sea salt, if necessary.

Preheat a large frying or sauté pan over a high heat and allow it to get extremely hot – do not rush this!

Meanwhile, drizzle the steak – on both sides – with olive oil and season well with salt. Add the steak to the hot pan and reduce the heat to medium-high. Fry for 3 minutes per side, adding butter when you flip the steak, and scooping the melted butter up over the steak. After this time I like to hold the steak with tongs, pressing the thick streak of fat against the pan for a minute – this will help to render the fat a little and crisp it up to make it much more delicious. Set the steak onto the chopping board to rest for a minute or two.

Add the pak choi to the pan, frying it for a minute or so per side, until charred and the dark green leaves are just wilted. Slice the steak and serve with the pak choi, well coated in chimichurri.

Saltimbocca Stroganoff
with Pan-fried Potatoes

This recipe came to me by divine intervention. In a rush to make pork saltimbocca for dinner, I came to learn that my sage plant had been the victim of a terrible storm. Desperate to salvage supper, I had to use what little I had left in my kitchen (we'd just packed to move home) and all I could find was brandy, paprika and a little cream. I'm so grateful.

Saltimbocca is normally made with veal. It's simply an escalope, wrapped in prosciutto and fried with wine or marsala. The title loosely translates to 'jump in the mouth', but this version reaches further – this will dance on your tastebuds.

Serves 1

60g (2¼oz) unsalted butter

1 tbsp sunflower oil

1 Maris Piper potato, cut into
   1cm (½in) dice

1 pork loin steak

2 slices prosciutto ham

100g (3½oz) chestnut mushrooms,
   finely sliced

½ tsp paprika

2 tbsp brandy or vodka

50ml (2fl oz) double cream

Fine sea salt and freshly ground black pepper

1 tbsp chopped chives, to serve

Start with the potatoes. Put half of the butter and the oil into a large, deep-sided frying or sauté pan and set over a high heat. Once the butter melts and starts to sputter, throw in the potato chunks and reduce the heat to medium. Fry the spuds, tossing or stirring every so often, for a good 20 minutes, or until golden, crispy and cooked through.

Meanwhile, prepare the pork. If the loin steak has a thick streak of fat running down the side, remove it. Put the steak between two pieces of cling film and bash it with a rolling pin or meat mallet until evenly thin. Wrap the slices of prosciutto around the piece of steak to cover both sides.

Once cooked, transfer the potatoes to a plate. Return the pan to a high heat and add the remaining butter. Once the butter melts and sputters, add the steak and mushrooms, and reduce the heat to medium. Fry the steak for 3 minutes per side, and give the mushrooms a stir every now and again.

When the steak is cooked, remove it from the pan, set aside on a plate and cover with foil to keep warm. Leaving the mushrooms in the pan, add the paprika and stir to coat the mushrooms. Throw in the brandy or vodka and allow it to bubble and evaporate. Add 100ml (3½fl oz) water and allow it to almost entirely evaporate, then remove from the heat and stir in the cream to a smooth sauce. Return the steaks to the pan, and coat them in the thick sauce. Throw in the potatoes. Season to taste with salt and pepper. Serve with the chopped chives scattered over the top.

Indo-Chinese Chilli Paneer

For such a speedy dish, this has such a developed profile of flavours and textures. More often than not, the green pepper and paneer is battered and deep-fried before being added to the spicy sauce, but I much prefer this version, which is cleaner and fresher in flavour. The key here is preparation and speed, so it's vital that everything is ready to go before you start cooking.

1 green pepper, deseeded and
    cut into 1cm (½in) chunks
2 spring onions, roughly chopped
1 red chilli, finely chopped
½ tsp chilli powder
15g (½oz) fresh ginger, peeled
    and finely grated
2 garlic cloves, minced

1 tbsp tomato ketchup
1 tbsp light soy sauce
1 tbsp honey
1 tsp cornflour
2 tbsp sunflower oil
100g (3½oz) paneer,
    cut into 1cm (½in) dice
Fine sea salt and black pepper

Serves 1

Put the green pepper and spring onions into one small bowl and have it handy. Put the chilli, chilli powder, ginger and garlic into another small bowl, and the ketchup, soy, honey, cornflour and 1 tablespoon of water into another small bowl.

Heat a small frying pan over a high heat and add 1 tablespoon of the oil. When the oil is hot, add the paneer and fry, tossing frequently, until it is golden and slightly crispy – a couple of minutes or so. Tip the paneer into a bowl and set aside until needed.

Return the pan to a high heat and add the remaining oil. When the oil is hot, add the pepper and onions and fry, tossing frequently, until the pepper is a little softer and the skin is slightly blistered – a couple of minutes.

Add the chilli, chilli powder, ginger and garlic and fry, stirring with a wooden spoon, just for a minute, then throw in the ketchup, soy, honey, cornflour and water and fry, stirring, for a few seconds until thickened. Remove the pan from the heat. If the mixture is very thick, add a tablespoon or so more water and stir to combine – the sauce should be like a thick honey.

Stir through the paneer, season to taste and serve.

Tahini and Miso Salmon with Soba Noodles

Although from disparate cultures, miso and tahini are a pairing of complete common sense. In much Japanese cookery miso is paired with sesame, which is precisely what tahini is: ground sesame seeds. Combined here with nutty buckwheat soba noodles and tender flakes of salmon, its delicacy is one that deserves dining solitude.

Serves 1

75g (2¾oz) soba noodles
1 tbsp light soy sauce,
    plus extra for serving
½ tbsp white rice vinegar
2 tsp brown miso paste
2 tsp tahini paste
2 tsp runny honey
1 tsp sesame oil

1 tbsp sunflower oil
2 spring onions,
    cut into 1cm (½in) chunks
2 baby courgettes,
    cut into 1cm (½in) discs
1 skinless, boneless salmon fillet,
    cut into chunks

Bring a medium pan of water to the boil and add the soba noodles. Cook for 5 minutes, or according to the packet instructions, then drain.

In a small bowl, whisk together the soy, vinegar, miso, tahini, honey, sesame oil and 1 teaspoon of water.

Heat a wok over a very high heat and add the sunflower oil. When the oil is hot and threatens to smoke, add the spring onions and courgettes and stir-fry for a minute. Add the salmon and fry until it is just pink in the middle, then throw in the drained soba noodles and cook for a further minute. Remove from the heat and toss through the miso-tahini mixture.

Drizzle with soy sauce to taste, and serve.

Szechuan Duck with Rainbow Chard and Cashews

Szechuan peppercorns are known as 'polarising peppercorns' in my family, because they seem to drive a great prickly wedge between us. I love them, and really rather enjoy their numbing qualities. The other interesting ingredients here are the ruby port and the black rice vinegar. The port I'm using simply because its sweetness complements duck, and the fortified flavour is resonant of a classic Shaoxing rice wine. The black rice vinegar is both sweet and acidic, and so works wonders here.

1 red chilli, finely sliced

30g (1oz) fresh ginger, peeled
   and minced

1 duck breast, skinned
   and finely sliced

2 tbsp ruby port

2 tbsp light soy sauce

2 tbsp black rice vinegar

2 tsp sesame oil

3 tbsp sunflower oil

½ tsp Szechuan peppercorns

50g (1¾oz) cashews

200g (7oz) rainbow chard,
   leaves roughly shredded,
   stalks cut into 1cm chunks

125g (4½oz) cooked brown rice

Fine sea salt

Fresh lime, to serve

Serves 1

Put the chilli and ginger into a mixing bowl and have it handy. Put the duck into another mixing bowl and season with a generous pinch of salt, tossing to coat the duck as evenly as possible. Put the ruby port, soy, vinegar and sesame oil into a third small bowl and have handy.

Heat a wok over a high heat and add the sunflower oil. When the oil gets so hot that it starts to smoke, add the chilli and ginger and stir-fry for a minute. Add the Szechuan peppercorns and fry for 30 seconds, then throw in the cashews and duck and fry for a minute or two, tossing, until the duck is just about seared on both sides. Add the chard and brown rice and fry, still tossing, until the chard wilts down.

Toss in the liquids and allow them to bubble and almost entirely evaporate. Remove from the heat and finish with a squeeze of fresh lime.

Corn Chowder with Ricotta and Chilli Lemon Oil

This simple bowlful is the perfect example of comfort food for one: a peppery, starchy soup studded with bursting corn kernels and tender pieces of potato. While I love the creaminess of corn chowder, this version is somewhat lifted by the chilli lemon oil and the floating island of ricotta.

Serves 1

1 tbsp rapeseed oil

1 banana shallot, finely chopped

1 small potato, finely diced

198g (7oz) can sweetcorn, drained

½ chicken stock cube

150ml whole milk

½ tbsp plain flour

Fine sea salt and coarse
    black pepper

For the oil

2 tbsp extra virgin olive oil

Zest of ½ unwaxed lemon

½ fat green chilli, finely sliced

To serve

100g (3½oz) ricotta

20g (¾oz) Parmesan, grated

A few parsley leaves

Set a medium saucepan over a medium-high heat and add the rapeseed oil. When the oil is hot, add the shallot, potato, sweetcorn and a generous pinch of salt and fry, stirring frequently, for 15 minutes – the shallot and potato should soften. Crumble in the stock cube, then pour in 150ml (5fl oz) water and half of the milk and bring to the boil, then reduce to a simmer and cook for a further 5 minutes.

Meanwhile, mix together the remaining milk and the flour in a small bowl to create a paste. When the soup has simmered for 5 minutes, add the paste and stir in, then cook for a further minute or two until the soup has thickened. Remove from the heat and cover.

Put a small saucepan over a high heat and add the olive oil. When the oil is hot, add the lemon zest and chilli and fry just for a minute to infuse the oil with the spice. Remove from the heat.

Add plenty of pepper to the chowder and ladle into a bowl. Top with the scoop of ricotta, allowing it to float like an island, and finish with a scattering of Parmesan, a few fresh parsley leaves, the chillies and drizzle with the oil.

Sweet and Sour Sprout and Bacon Curry

*Curries, for the most part, conjure images of great gatherings fuelled by energy and chatter.
Much as I love that idea of a banquet of spice, there's something consoling about a single panful
of curry containing just enough for one. If I find myself alone on a weekend, I'll be sure to make
something along these lines, to be accompanied by a bottle of Gewürztraminer or Riesling.*

1 tbsp sunflower oil

150g (5oz) Brussels sprouts,
    finely sliced

1 small onion, finely sliced

80g (3oz) smoked bacon lardons

2 garlic cloves, minced

2.5cm (1 in) piece ginger,
    peeled and finely grated

½ tsp ground cumin

½ tsp ground coriander

½ tsp chilli powder

1 cardamom pod, bruised

1 tbsp dark soy sauce

2 tbsp lemon juice

1 tbsp agave nectar or honey

125ml (4fl oz) water

Fine sea salt

Serves 1

Set a large, deep-sided frying or sauté pan over a medium heat. Once the pan is hot add the
oil, sprouts, onion and bacon and fry, stirring occasionally, for 15 minutes – the onion should
soften and perhaps colour, but only slightly.

Add the garlic, ginger, cumin, coriander, chilli powder and cardamom and stir-fry for just a
minute until everything smells strongly. Throw in the soy, lemon juice and agave or honey, and
stir to combine, then add the water and allow to come to a simmer. Simmer for 5 minutes, then
season to taste. Remove the cardamom pod. Decant into a bowl and devour in perfect solitude.

Burnt Butter, Sage and Blue Cheese Omelette

As far as I have encountered, there are two camps of omelette makers. In the first camp, the eggs are cooked gently over a low heat and fiddled with using a rubber spatula. There's nothing wrong with that, but I find the eggs always end up a little rubbery when cooked in that way. I'm in the more traditional French camp, where the pan is allowed to get very hot before the eggs are added and then thrashed about until they set. This is a much quicker method and the result is a far more tender omelette.

Serves 1

3 large eggs
40g (1½oz) unsalted butter
4 sage leaves, roughly chopped, plus a
   few extra whole ones to serve
Fine sea salt

To serve
40g (1½oz) Dolcelatte cheese,
   crumbled
Freshly ground black pepper

Set a large frying pan over a high heat and allow it to get hot. Meanwhile, crack the eggs into a mixing bowl, add a hefty pinch of salt and whisk until well mixed and very loose.

Put half the butter into the pan and allow it to melt and bubble fiercely. Add the chopped sage and toss about the pan, then throw in the beaten eggs. Keeping the pan on the heat, quickly shake the pan back and forth, which will drag the omelette all over the pan, like a rag blowing about in a gale. As the omelette sets, but maintains a little runniness, tilt the pan away from you, still shaking it, to coax the omelette to curl up in the edge furthest away from you. When it does, tip it onto a plate.

Return the pan to the heat and quickly throw in the remaining butter. Allow it to fizz and bubble and then burn, then add the whole sage leaves and fry until crispy. Pour the cooked butter over the omelette, and top with the crisp sage leaves. Finish with a scattering of crumbled cheese and some black pepper.

Blackened Garlic Soup

It's astounding that a very small handful of ingredients can create something as complexly delicious as this. This soup, based on the Provençal peasant soup aigo bouido, *is the very finest of tonics. For me, it brings instant calm. I blacken the garlic by frying it in hot oil for a few minutes, before slicing it, ready to infuse, into the water. This sweetens the garlic and tames its acrid tang. The key part to making this soup velvety is to incorporate an egg yolk mixed with oil. I can't stress enough, and will repeat myself below, that you must add the oil to the egg extremely cautiously to ensure it emulsifies. It isn't difficult, so don't be put off, but please give this recipe the tenderness it deserves. If you do, it will return the favour tenfold.*

Serves 1

3 tbsp extra virgin olive oil
3 fat garlic cloves, unpeeled
4 sage leaves
250ml (9fl oz) water

1 large egg yolk
Fine sea salt and freshly
ground black pepper

Heat a medium saucepan over a high heat and add 2 tablespoons of the oil. When the oil is hot and starts to ripple, add the garlic cloves and fry, turning only occasionally, until the skins are completely black – about 4 minutes. Remove and set onto a chopping board to cool for a minute or two. Decant the oil into a ramekin or mug and reserve.

When the garlic cloves are cool enough to handle, remove the blackened skins and discard. Some of the garlic flesh will probably be charred, too, but that's fine. Slice the cloves finely.

Return the pan to a medium-high heat and add the remaining 1 tablespoon of oil (not the oil you reserved). When the oil is hot, add the sliced garlic and the whole sage leaves, and allow them to crackle in the oil for just 30 seconds. Add the water, bring to the boil, then reduce to a very gentle simmer and cook for 10 minutes.

Meanwhile, put the egg yolk into a small mixing bowl. Whisking constantly, add the reserved oil a drop at a time, ensuring each inclusion is fully incorporated before adding the next. You should be left with a silky yellow emulsion.

Pour a splash of the garlic water onto the egg yolk mixture and whisk well to incorporate. Then pour that back into the pan, off the heat, and whisk constantly and with meaning until you have a smooth, velvety soup.

Season very generously with salt and pepper. The salt will transform this from an insipid water to a wholesome broth, whose flavour suggests it has been simmering for hours.

table for one

Mushroom Pho

Pho, the Vietnamese noodle broth, is one of my go-to cold remedies. It is spicy, it is nutritious and it is packed with flavour. Ordinarily it is made with rice noodles, but I prefer wholewheat for its nuttiness. The porcini mushrooms not only add a meaty texture but also their musty tone is imparted into the water before the broth is simmered, which only serves to amplify the flavour.

1 nest (about 40g/1½oz)
  wholewheat noodles

For the broth
20g (¾oz) dried porcini mushrooms
500ml (18fl oz) boiling water
1 beef stock pot
30g (1oz) fresh ginger,
  peeled and finely sliced
1 garlic clove, finely sliced
1 star anise

2 cardamom pods,
  bruised
½ red chilli, sliced
2 tsp light soy sauce
1 tsp fish sauce
1 spring onion, roughly chopped
Small handful of baby spinach,
  roughly chopped
Small handful of coriander,
  roughly chopped
1 tsp black sesame seeds

Serves 1

First soak the porcini mushrooms. Put them into a mixing bowl and pour over the boiling water. Leave to soak while you prepare the noodles.

Fill a small saucepan with water, bring to a boil and cook the noodles according to the packet instructions – usually about 5 minutes. Drain when cooked, and keep the noodles in the dry pan, off the heat.

Drain the mushrooms, catching the soaking water in a medium saucepan and setting the mushrooms on the chopping board out of the way. Add the stock pot, ginger, garlic, star anise, cardamom pods, chilli, soy sauce, fish sauce and spring onion to the pan. Bring to the boil, then reduce to a simmer and cook for 15 minutes.

Put the noodles into a serving bowl, add a little chopped spinach and coriander and the mushrooms, then pour over the stock (with or without the aromatics – I'm happy to navigate my way around them, but some may be a little fussier). Finish with a sprinkling of sesame seeds. Slurp and sip in solitary serenity.

Broken Eggs with Potatoes
and Serrano Ham

From childhood, we are taught to fear the falling egg. From nursery rhymes and school sports days, we develop a need to treat the delicate capsules with utmost respect. At the checkouts, we inspect their shells with forensic attention and nestle them atop the shopping bag. This recipe is one of the rare instances in which Humpty Dumpty's descent would have ended deliciously; it's precisely the explosive breaking of the yolk that defines this dish.

Serves 1

2 slices of Serrano ham

1 tbsp olive oil

1 new potato, finely sliced

1 garlic clove, finely sliced

4 cherry tomatoes, roughly chopped

1 spring onion, finely sliced

1 tbsp sliced black olives

3 large eggs

Small handful of parsley, roughly chopped

Tabasco sauce, for drizzling

Sea salt flakes and coarse black pepper

Fresh bread, to serve

Heat a medium, deep-sided frying or sauté pan with a lid over a medium heat. Once the pan is hot, add the Serrano ham slices and fry for 30 seconds or so per side, until brown and a little crispier. Remove from the pan and set aside.

Heat the oil in the same pan over a medium heat. Add the potato slices and fry for 8–10 minutes, flipping once, until golden. Add the garlic, tomatoes, spring onion and olives, and stir-fry for a minute or two. Season well with sea salt flakes at this stage, so that the base ingredients are all as flavourful as possible.

Make three clearings in the pan for the eggs. Break the eggs and, holding them about 30cm above the pan, allow each egg to fall from the shell, crashing into the dents in the tomato mixture. Quickly season each egg with a little salt and pepper, then pop on the lid and cook just until the whites are softly set and the yolks remain runny.

Finish with a scattering of chopped parsley and a drizzle of Tabasco sauce. Place the fried ham slices on top and dig in, mopping up the sauce with chunks of fresh bread.

meat free

Part-time Vegetarian

I come from a farming family. The bloodline of our Friesian herd dates back to 1919, when my great-grandfather was given his first four cows: a gift from his own father to help him find his feet after fighting in the war. Most of our 160 cows are direct descendants of those four girls.

My first job, at a tender age, was to feed the calves each morning; something I detested but was obliged to do. There weren't any excuses, and the parental sick notes that would come to exonerate me from most physical education throughout high school wouldn't cut it here – my parents were, after all, my bosses. Before first light, I'd zip my sleepy self into overalls and drag my feet across the yard. In the dim glow of the bare barn bulb, as the wind battered the corrugated walls, I'd see to the calves. I'd feed them their milk. I'd sit on the scratching bales and watch as they guzzled the food. Their demanding bleats and stamping hooves would calm as they filled their aching bellies.

What that forced labour gifted me with is a love of nature; although I think most humans are born with an intrinsic appreciation of the great outdoors. That's why after a hot dry spell the first drops of rain smell so welcoming to us. We are sensitive to that petrichor: the scent of rain on hot, dusty ground. Sadly, and as a side note, this valuable time in the open air is something that too many children these days are not getting. Apparently, 75 per cent of kids in the UK get less fresh air than prisoners.

In the time spent outdoors and on farms, we are taught about produce. We witness the growing of crops and the rearing of cattle: an ancient industry that far predates the Industrial Revolution. Deep in labyrinthine fields of corn we see the world. Through the bleating of sticky newborn calves, we see life. As those crops grow from dirt, as new life lands heavily and with a thud in the dewy field, we learn to respect our planet and the flora and fauna it gives us.

All life is precious. If we kill an animal for food, we know where it comes from. We should know that every part of that beast will be put to use. But that isn't currently the case. The meat industry is out of control. In one year, worldwide, 50 billion animals are reared and killed for food (that's about seven animals per person per year). Furthermore – and I don't wish to harp on too much, but you'll understand I have a point to make – harnessing grain to feed animals only serves to hike up the price of that grain, making it harder for the impoverished on our planet to find food. Consider that, along with the quantity of water used to cultivate this grain and the gasses created in industrialised meat production, and it's clear to see that we are waging war on our own planet.

I'm not proselytising here, nor am I forming an aggressive vegan campaign to smite all meat eaters. I am a meat eater. I will continue to eat meat for the rest of my life. Our anatomies have evolved from the cooking and eating of meat: pronounced and heavy jaws, filled with meat-tearing teeth, no longer weigh us down. Our brains are bigger. We can derive vital fat-soluble vitamins from meat – but those are vitamins that we simply don't need every single day.

My step-father, up until his 60s, was a carnivore: haggis or kippers for breakfast, beef butties for lunch, steak for dinner. But even his bloodthirstiness is receding as the meat industry swells and starts to buckle our planet. And I am following suit. It seems that the old mantra of our grandmothers rings true: everything in moderation.

Black Tarka Salad

Tarka dhal is one of my favourite comfort foods, and this salad is a lunchtime spin on that. A tarka is a blend of spices and aromatics that is cooked in hot oil then thrown into the main dish. This is delicious a day or two later, so do hoard a lunchbox-full, deep in the fridge.

Serves 2–4

For the salad

400g (14oz) can chickpeas
  (preferably black chickpeas)
400g (14oz) can black beans
250g (9oz) pouch of cooked
  beluga lentils
Small handful of coriander,
  roughly chopped
Juice of ½ lime

For the tarka

50ml (2fl oz) sunflower oil
1 green chilli, finely chopped
1 small red onion, finely chopped
3 garlic cloves, minced
30g (1oz) fresh ginger, peeled
  and finely grated
1 tsp black mustard seeds
2 tsp cumin seeds
1 tsp nigella seeds
10 dried curry leaves
1 tsp fine sea salt

Drain the chickpeas, beans and lentils and toss them together in a large mixing bowl with the coriander and lime juice.

Heat the oil in a medium saucepan over a high heat. Once the oil is hot, add all the ingredients for the tarka, except the salt. Fry, stirring, just until the seeds start to pop violently – about a minute. Pour the tarka straight into the bowl with the beans, add the salt, and stir together.

Golden Rice and Black Lentil Salad

Rice has to be one of the ultimate conveyors of flavour. It seems to willingly accept and proudly purvey just about any combination that is thrown at it. This salad is golden and glorious, and is perfect for grazing upon during long summer evenings.

2 tbsp olive oil

1 red onion, finely chopped

1 tsp nigella seeds

1 tsp cumin seeds

2 green chillies, finely chopped

2 garlic cloves, minced

200g (7oz) basmati rice

1 tsp ground turmeric

250g (9oz) pouch of cooked beluga lentils

1 yellow pepper, deseeded and finely chopped

3 plum tomatoes, finely chopped

Small handful of parsley, roughly chopped

Juice of 1 lime

1–2 tsp fine sea salt

For the dressing

6 tbsp Greek yogurt

1 garlic clove, minced

2 tbsp olive oil

Serves 4

Heat a medium saucepan (one you have a lid for) over a high heat. When the pan is hot, add the oil and reduce the heat to medium-high. Once the oil is hot and starts to shimmer, add the onion, nigella and cumin seeds and fry, stirring frequently, for a few minutes, until the onion is lightly coloured and has softened. Add the chillies and garlic and fry for a few seconds, then throw in the rice and ground turmeric. Pour water into the pan – enough to cover the rice by 2cm (¾in). Allow the water to come to the boil, then pop on the lid and cook for 9 minutes. Remove the pan from the heat but keep it covered for an extra 5 minutes to steam the rice.

When the rice has steamed, fluff it up with a fork and pour it into a large mixing or salad bowl. Toss the rice together with the lentils, pepper, tomatoes, parsley and lime juice and season with salt to taste – it'll need a good teaspoon or two.

Make the dressing by mixing together the yogurt, garlic and olive oil in a small mixing bowl. Drizzle the dressing over the rice salad and serve.

Spelt Pancakes with Whipped Goat's Cheese, Beetroot, Radish and Buckwheat

This goes against the stereotypical stack of pancakes, towering high and sodden with maple syrup. While there is always a very welcome place for that version, this savoury twist feels much more wholesome. The spelt flour and toasted buckwheat – which, by the way, are sold in most supermarkets if you look hard enough – offer a nuttiness to the classic combination of goat's cheese and beetroot.

Serves 2-4

For the pancake batter
260g (9¼oz) wholemeal spelt flour
1 tsp fine sea salt
1 tsp baking powder
4 large eggs
150ml (5fl oz) whole milk
2 tbsp sunflower oil

To assemble
1 tbsp buckwheat
100g (3½oz) soft goat's cheese
100g (3½oz) Greek yogurt
2 cooked baby beetroots, finely sliced
4 radishes, finely sliced
Small handful of purple radish sprouts
Drizzle of runny honey

For the batter, put the flour, salt and baking powder into a mixing bowl and whisk together. In a jug, beat together the eggs and milk, then pour into the dry ingredients, whisking constantly, until you have a smooth, thick batter.

Heat a large frying pan over a medium-high heat. Once the pan is hot, wipe it with a little oil on a piece of kitchen paper. Add dollops of the batter to form pancakes of about 6cm (2½in) in diameter – I got eight pancakes in total from the batter. (You will need to do this in batches.) Fry for a minute or so, until pinprick bubbles form, then flip and fry for just 30 seconds more. Stack the cooked pancakes on a plate or chopping board.

Return the pan to a high heat and add the buckwheat. Toast, shaking the pan back and forth, for a minute or so, until the buckwheat smells nutty and is crunchy to the bite. Remove from the heat and set aside.

In a mixing bowl, whisk together the goat's cheese and Greek yogurt until softened.

Serve the pancake stack with the cheese mixture dolloped on the side. Top the pancakes with the beetroots, radishes and sprouts. Drizzle the finished towers of pancake with runny honey and scatter with the toasted buckwheat.

Beetroot and Freekeh Salad with Tangerine and Tahini Dressing

Salads need a variety of flavours and textures to be just right. In this offering, there is the earthiness of beetroot, the sweetness of the tangerine, the bitter nuttiness of the tahini, all rounded together with salty feta and sweet-yet-sharp cranberries. Freekeh is simply young, green wheat that is toasted (sometimes fired) and is similar to bulgar wheat or barley. Don't be put off by the unusual name; it is so simple to cook.

Serves 4

75g (2¾oz) pecans
200g (7oz) wholegrain freekeh
1 small golden beetroot
1 candy beetroot
75g (2¾oz) dried cranberries
100g (3½oz) feta cheese

For the dressing
2 tbsp tahini
Juice of 2 tangerines
2 tbsp olive oil
2 tsp red wine vinegar
Fine sea salt and
    freshly ground black pepper

Heat the saucepan over a high heat. Once hot, add the pecans and fry for just a minute or so, until they release their nutty aroma. Chop them roughly, and throw them into a large mixing or salad bowl.

Put the freekeh into the saucepan along with 1 litre (1¾ pints) of water. Set the pan over a high heat and bring to the boil, then reduce to a simmer and cook for 20 minutes.

Meanwhile, peel and finely slice the beetroot – if you have a mandolin, use that, or a very sharp knife. Put the beetroot and the cranberries into the mixing bowl with the pecans, and crumble in the feta. Toss together.

For the dressing, simply stir together the tahini, tangerine juice, olive oil and red wine vinegar in a small mixing bowl, along with a pinch of salt and pepper to taste.

Once the freekeh is tender and cooked, drain away the water – I use a sieve – and allow to cool slightly before adding to the beetroot. Toss the salad together, tip it out onto a plate, then drizzle over the dressing just before serving.

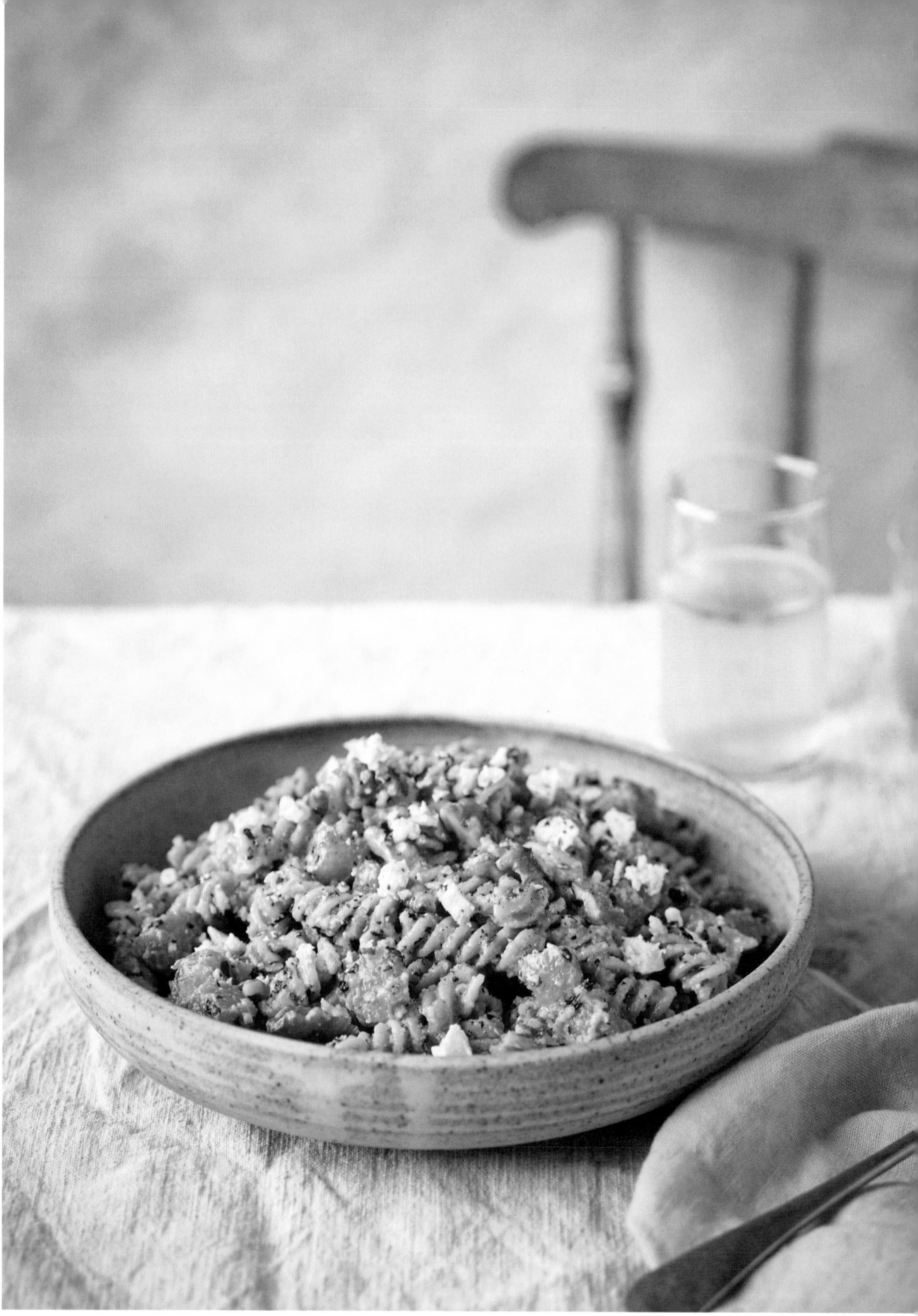

Walnut, Feta and Mint Pesto with Sweet Potato and Wholewheat Pasta

Speedy though this may be, it feels as if it'll do you a lifetime of good. I love the combination here, it's all so earthy yet it is somehow revived by the mint and the sweetness of the potato. While this will serve two, I have eaten a full batch myself – but I daren't measure my greed against that of others.

200g (7oz) dried wholewheat fusilli
1 large sweet potato,
   peeled and cut into 1cm (½in) dice
Fine sea salt

For the pesto
60g (2¼oz) walnuts
Handful of mint leaves
50g (1¾oz) feta cheese, plus extra to top
150ml (5fl oz) rapeseed oil
Freshly ground black pepper

Serves 2

First toast the walnuts: heat a medium saucepan over a high heat. Once hot, add the walnuts and fry, shaking the pan occasionally, for a minute or so, just until the walnuts release their bittersweet aroma. Set aside.

Fill the pan about half-full with well-salted water and bring it to the boil. Drop in the pasta and sweet potato and boil for 8 minutes.

Meanwhile, carry on with the pesto. If you're using a mini food-processor, put everything into it all together, along with ½ teaspoon fine salt, and pulse to a chunky pesto. If you're doing this in a pestle and mortar, it's best to pound the mint leaves with the salt, then add the walnuts and feta and pound until chunky. Add the pepper and oil last and blend to combine.

When the pasta is cooked, drain it but reserve 2 tablespoons of the starchy cooking water and add that to the pesto. Return the pasta to the pan, off the heat, and stir through the pesto. Serve with a scattering of crumbled feta and a pinch of salt to taste.

Halloumi with Honey and Sesame Seeds

When holidaying on Zakynthos a couple of years ago, we visited, on the recommendation of the entire town, the Halfway House restaurant in Tsilivi. While the name suggests it might be run by some British expats, longing to enthral the Mediterranean palate with the English Fry-Up, it's actually owned by a Zakynthian lad and his family. This dish is on the menu there, as it is in many Greek restaurants, and was the best version I've tried.

Serves 2

2 tsp of mixed black and white sesame seeds

3 tbsp runny honey

225–250g (8–9oz) block of halloumi

2 tbsp olive oil

Pinch of dried oregano

Set a small frying pan over a high heat. Once the pan is hot, add the sesame seeds and toast for a minute, until the seeds are ever so slightly darker. Remove from the frying pan and set aside.

Put the honey into a small saucepan and set over a medium heat, allowing it to warm up while you prepare the halloumi.

Cut the halloumi in half horizontally, so you end up with two large slabs. Heat the frying pan over a medium-high heat and add the oil. Once the oil is hot and starts to shimmer, add the halloumi slabs and fry for a few minutes per side, until mottled with char.

Serve the halloumi on a plate, drizzled with the warm honey, and finish with a scattering of sesame seeds and dried oregano.

Squash, Mushroom and Amaretti Panzanella

Albeit peculiar, this isn't a combination I have devised. It is a very popular filling for ravioli and tortelli in Emilia-Romagna, Italy. It's an assortment of ingredients that I absolutely love, and used in my last book, Comfort, *with sweet potato gnocchi. This version, an evolution of that, is slightly lighter, and is the perfect way to use up stale bread. On that note, the rye bread here does not refer to that thinly sliced pumpernickel, which never seems to go stale. This requires an actual loaf made with either rye or spelt, the nuttiness of which only serves to amplify the flavour; though if all you have is stale white, just use that.*

100g (3½oz) kale, roughly chopped

60g (2¼oz) pumpkin seeds

200g (7oz) stale rye bread,
    cut into 2cm (¾in) cubes

2 tbsp olive oil

500g (18oz) butternut squash,
    peeled and cut into 1cm (½in) dice

250g (9oz) chestnut mushrooms, sliced

6 sage leaves, roughly chopped

100g (3½oz) Dolcelatte

2 amaretti biscuits, crushed

For the dressing

4 tbsp cider vinegar

4 tbsp extra virgin olive oil

Fine sea salt and
    freshly ground black pepper

Serves 4

Put the kale into a large mixing or salad bowl.

Heat a large frying pan over a high heat. Once hot, add the pumpkin seeds and fry, tossing the pan occasionally and allowing the seeds to pop, for a couple of minutes – usually they're mostly toasted when the popping starts to slow down. Add the seeds to the bowl with the kale. Throw the bread cubes into the pan and fry, tossing frequently, until crisp. Add to the bowl.

Return the pan to a high heat and when hot, add the oil, squash, mushrooms and sage, and reduce the heat to medium-high. Fry, tossing occasionally, for 10 minutes or so, until the squash is cooked through and the mushrooms are soft and slightly coloured. Pour the squash mixture into the salad bowl while it is still hot – the residual heat will help to wilt the kale a little, reducing its overwhelming volume.

Make the dressing by mixing together the vinegar and olive oil with a generous pinch of salt and pepper. Pour the dressing over the salad, then add dollops of the Dolcelatte cheese. Finish by crumbling over the crushed amaretti biscuits.

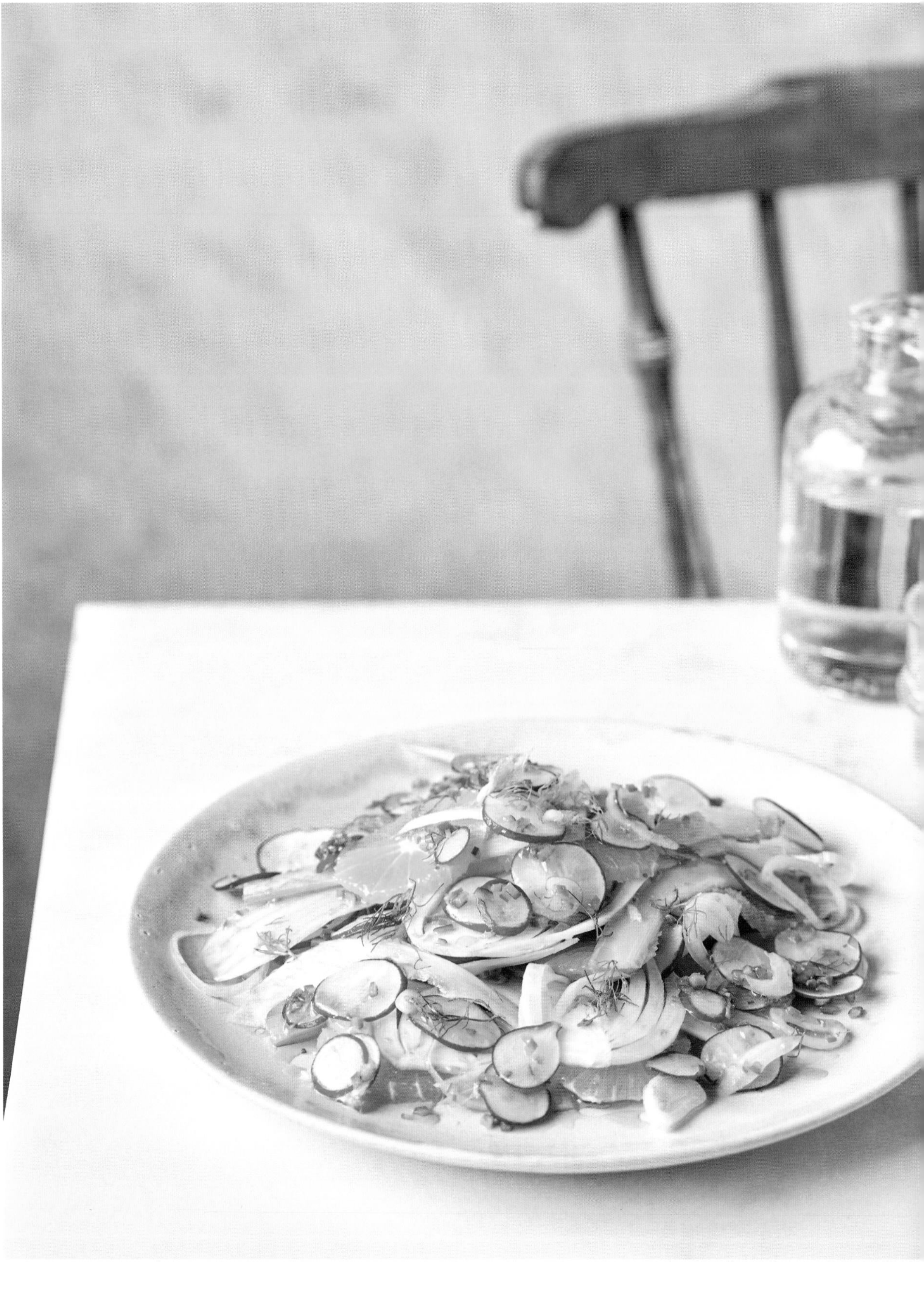

Fennel, Radish, Orange and Chilli Salad

This is such a refreshing salad and is so easily thrown together. It makes for a great light lunch, but is also superb served as part of a larger spread.

1 large fennel bulb

100g (3½oz) radishes, very finely sliced

1 banana shallot, sliced into fine rings

2 tbsp red wine vinegar

1 tbsp orange blossom honey

2 small oranges

1 green chilli, very finely chopped

1 tbsp extra virgin olive oil

Sea salt flakes

Serves 2-4

Remove the fronds from the fennel (save them for later), slice the bulb as finely as possible – I use a mandolin, but you can just use a very sharp knife – and put it into a large mixing or salad bowl. Add the radishes and shallot to the bowl along with the vinegar, honey, the juice from one of the oranges and a generous pinch of salt.

Add the chilli to the bowl along with the zest of the other orange. Peel the orange and slice it finely. Serve the salad layered with the oranges, then scatter over the reserved fennel fronds and drizzle over the oil.

Aubergine Katsu Curry

Katsu curry, the Tokyo classic, is a breaded cutlet (usually pork or chicken) served with curry sauce. While I love chicken, I find aubergine to be an even better counterpart to that mildly spiced curry sauce, as its flesh acts like a sponge and soaks up much more flavour.

Serves 4

For the curry
2 tbsp vegetable oil
1 onion, finely chopped
2 carrots, finely chopped
2.5cm (1in) piece of fresh ginger,
    peeled and finely grated
3 garlic cloves, minced
2 tbsp plain flour
1 tbsp mild curry powder
2 tsp light soy sauce
1 tbsp dark soy sauce
600ml (1 pint) vegetable stock
1 tbsp mango chutney
1 tbsp tomato ketchup

For the aubergine
75g (2¾oz) plain flour
4 large eggs
300g (10½oz) panko breadcrumbs,
    bashed to fine crumbs
2 aubergines, cut into
    2cm (¾in)-thick discs
4 tbsp vegetable oil
Fine sea salt

To serve
Cooked white rice
Pea shoots (optional)

For the curry, heat the vegetable oil in a medium saucepan over a high heat. Once the oil is hot, add the onion, carrots and ginger and stir for a minute or so, until the onions start to look like they are becoming dry. Reduce the heat to medium and cook until soft – about 10 minutes – stirring occasionally to prevent sticking. Stir in the garlic, then add the flour and curry powder, stir-frying for a minute. Increase the heat to high and add the soy sauces and stock. Allow the curry to come to a boil, then reduce to a simmer and cook until reduced by a third. Remove from the heat and stir in the mango chutney and ketchup.

Meanwhile, prepare the aubergine. Put the flour into a deep rimmed plate, beat the eggs in another and scatter the breadcrumbs onto a third. Season each plate with salt. Season the aubergine slices with salt, dip them into the flour until well coated, then into the egg, and finally into the breadcrumbs – make sure you get all sides of the aubergine coated.

Heat the oil in a large, deep-sided frying or sauté pan over a medium heat. Once the oil is hot, add the aubergine pieces and fry on each side until a deep, rich golden brown. Remove from the oil and put onto a plate lined with kitchen paper to blot dry.

Serve the pieces of aubergine with rice and the curry sauce and finish with pea shoots, if using.

Sweet Potato and Harissa Salad

Harissa paste, that Moroccan stalwart, is something I hoard jars of in my cupboards. Whether slicked over chicken thighs, marinated into steaks or used simply to add spice and zing to roast potatoes, it's something I would now struggle to part with. It is delicious in this salad with the sweet potatoes and pungent goat's cheese.

Serves 2

75g (2¾oz) sunflower seeds

2 tbsp olive oil

2 medium sweet potatoes,
    peeled and cut into 2cm (¾in) dice

2 tbsp rose harissa paste

100g (3½oz) goat's cheese

1 small red onion, finely sliced

Small handful of mint, roughly chopped

4 radishes, finely sliced

1 small orange, peeled and segmented

Extra virgin olive oil

Sea salt flakes

Heat a large frying pan over a medium-high heat. Once the pan is hot, add the sunflower seeds and toast, shaking the pan back and forth, for a minute or so until the seeds release their earthy aroma. Tip into a small bowl and set aside until needed.

Return the pan to a medium-high heat and add the olive oil. Once the oil is hot and starts to shimmer, add the sweet potato pieces and fry, tossing occasionally, for 15–20 minutes, until the sweet potato is tender enough to eat, and is slightly charred. Add the harissa and toss through the potatoes, still on the heat, for a minute or so. Remove from the heat and allow to cool.

Tip the cooled pieces of harissa-slicked sweet potato into a large mixing bowl and crumble in the goat's cheese. Add the onion, almost all the mint and the radishes, and toss together. Season to taste.

Serve the salad with orange segments on top, a drizzling of extra virgin olive oil, and scatter with the remaining chopped mint.

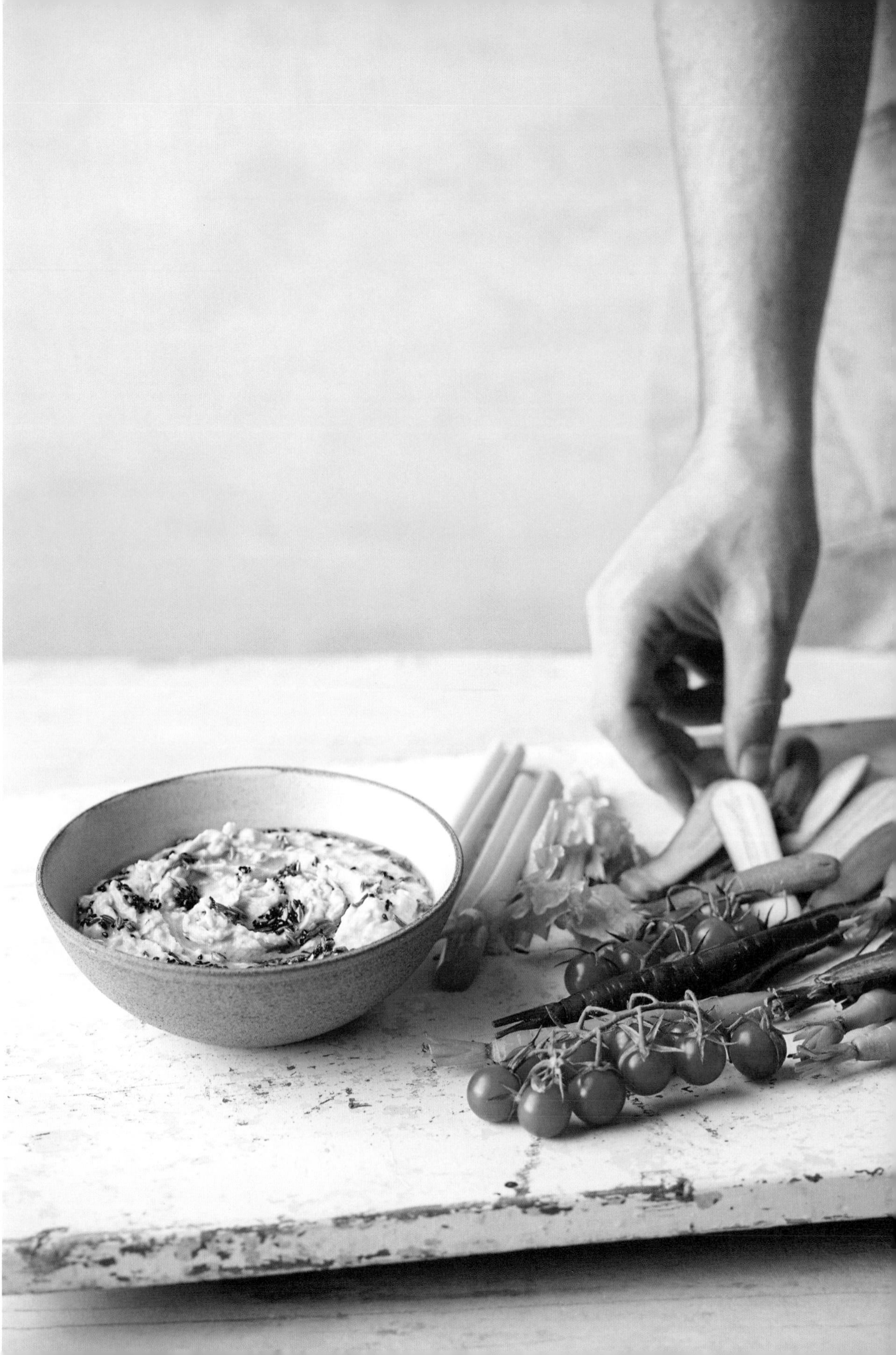

Roquefort Hummus with Nigella and Fennel Oil

As a food writer, it can be difficult to come up with new ideas. There's a vast number of wonderful food books in the world, and more often than not an idea will already have been done. One thing I always tell people who ask the classic question of, 'Where do your ideas come from?' is that it's often about perspective. When I look at an ingredient that might already be considered to be complete – like a container of hummus – I think, 'How can that be improved?'

This recipe might seem like it's just been thrown together with scraps leftover in the fridge, but it actually took a few attempts to get quite right. It lifts the classic union of hummus and carrot sticks to something more indulgent and developed in flavour.

200g (7oz) hummus

100g (3½oz) Roquefort, at room temperature

2 tbsp olive oil

¼ tsp fennel seeds

¼ tsp nigella seeds

2 tsp pomegranate molasses

Makes 200g (7oz)

Put the hummus and Roquefort into a mixing bowl and whisk together until fairly smooth.

Heat a medium saucepan over a high heat and add the oil. When the oil is hot, add the fennel and nigella seeds and fry, just for 30 seconds or so, until the seeds are fragrant. Pour half of the oil and seed mixture onto the hummus and mix in, tip the rest out into a bowl and set aside.

When ready to serve, decant the hummus into a serving bowl. Drizzle the remaining oil and seed mixture on top, and finish with a drizzle of pomegranate molasses.

Asparagus Tempura with Porcini Mayo

When asparagus season arrives, the tapering country lanes normally dotted with dog walkers, cyclists and suicidal pheasants become littered with A-frame blackboards from the local farm shops: Formby asparagus has arrived. The roads transform from commuter pathways to racetracks, as we all fight for the pick of the bunch. Its flavour is so pure, so clean, that little more than merely cooking it is needed. This recipe celebrates the flavour of asparagus, the mushroom tarragon dip complementing it perfectly.

Serves 2-4

For the asparagus

Sunflower oil, for deep-frying

55g (2oz) plain flour

50g (1¾oz) cornflour

½ tsp bicarbonate of soda

½ tsp white or cider vinegar

250g (9oz) asparagus
   (the thicker the better)

Fine sea salt

For the mayonnaise

15g (½oz) dried porcini mushrooms

175ml (6fl oz) recently boiled water

100g (3½oz) mayonnaise

2 tbsp chopped tarragon

Fine black pepper

First soak the porcini mushrooms. Put them into a mixing bowl and pour over the recently boiled water. Allow the mushrooms to soak for 5 minutes.

Fill a wok with sunflower oil so that there is a decent depth in which you can fry the asparagus. Set this over a medium-high heat and allow it to get hot.

Meanwhile, in a second bowl put the flour, cornflour, bicarbonate of soda and a pinch of salt and whisk to combine. When the mushrooms have soaked, set a sieve over the bowl of flour and pour over the mushroom water, catching the mushrooms in the sieve. Whisk the water into the flour vigorously to create a smooth batter. Add the vinegar and whisk in.

Chop the mushrooms finely and return them to their soaking bowl, then add the mayonnaise, chopped tarragon and a generous pinch of black pepper. Beat to combine.

Snap off the woody ends from the asparagus, then, in batches, dunk them into the batter and pop them into the hot oil. Fry for a minute or so until golden, then remove from the oil – I use kitchen tongs – and place onto a clean tea towel to blot away excess oil. Repeat until all of the asparagus is battered.

Serve the asparagus with the mayonnaise, and dunk away.

Sriracha Devilled Eggs

I make no bones about the fact that I adore sriracha. I can squeeze it onto almost anything – especially hard-boiled eggs – and devour it with nothing short of greedy glee. This recipe is a slightly more sophisticated version of an elevenses snack that I enjoy regularly.

6 large eggs
Ice, for cooling
4 tbsp mayonnaise
2 tbsp sriracha
4 chives, finely sliced
Fine sea salt

For the crumb
15g (½oz) unsalted butter
30g (1oz) breadcrumbs
1 garlic clove
2 tsp black sesame seeds

Makes 12

Bring a medium saucepan of water to the boil. Once the water is at a rolling boil, gently place the eggs into it and cook for 12 minutes. Meanwhile, prepare a mixing bowl of iced water. When the eggs have cooked for 12 minutes, immediately remove them from the hot water with a slotted spoon, place into the iced water and allow to cool for a few minutes.

Meanwhile, prepare the crumb. Set a large frying pan over a high heat and add the butter. When it melts add the breadcrumbs, whole garlic clove and sesame seeds, and toast, stirring, until crispy. Remove the pan from the heat and pluck out the garlic.

When the eggs are cool enough to handle, peel, then slice them lengthways. Carefully remove the yolks – I find a teaspoon to be the best utensil. Empty the mixing bowl of its iced water and quickly dry it, then put the yolks into that. Add the mayonnaise and sriracha and beat until smooth. Season to taste.

Put the yolk mixture into a piping bag fitted with a star nozzle and pipe the filling back into each egg half. Finish with a scattering of chives and the breadcrumbs.

Black Pepper and Basil Vegetable Stir-fry

This recipe should come with a warning: it is intensely hot. But it's not a chilli heat that commands vats of cooling ice water, rather the more nasal, slightly tangy heat, that you'd only expect of black pepper. There's something ascetic about it – pleasure from pain – because although this is only for the most fearless of diners, the combination of black pepper and basil is wonderful.

Serves 2

2 tbsp olive oil

1 aubergine, cut into 2cm (¾in) dice

4 spring onions,
    sliced into 2cm (¾in) pieces

½ courgette, cut into 1cm (½in) discs

2 banana shallots, cut into
    8 segments lengthwise

40g (1½oz) fresh ginger, peeled and
    finely grated

4 garlic cloves, finely sliced

1 fat red chilli, finely sliced

2 tbsp light soy sauce

4 tbsp dark soy sauce

1 tbsp dark brown sugar

1 tsp cornflour

2 tsp freshly ground black pepper

Handful of basil leaves,
    roughly chopped

Freshly squeezed lime juice, to serve

Set a large frying pan over a medium heat and add the oil. Once the oil shimmers, add the aubergine, spring onions, courgette, banana shallots, ginger, garlic and red chilli. Fry, stirring only occasionally, until the vegetables are softened and ever so slightly browned – about 15 minutes.

Meanwhile, combine the soy sauces, sugar and cornflour in a small bowl, stirring to dissolve the sugar into the liquid.

Once the vegetables have cooked, increase the heat to medium-high and throw in the pepper. Toss together for just a moment, then add the soy sauce mixture and allow it to bubble and thicken for a minute. Remove from the heat, stir the basil through, and serve with a squeeze of lime juice.

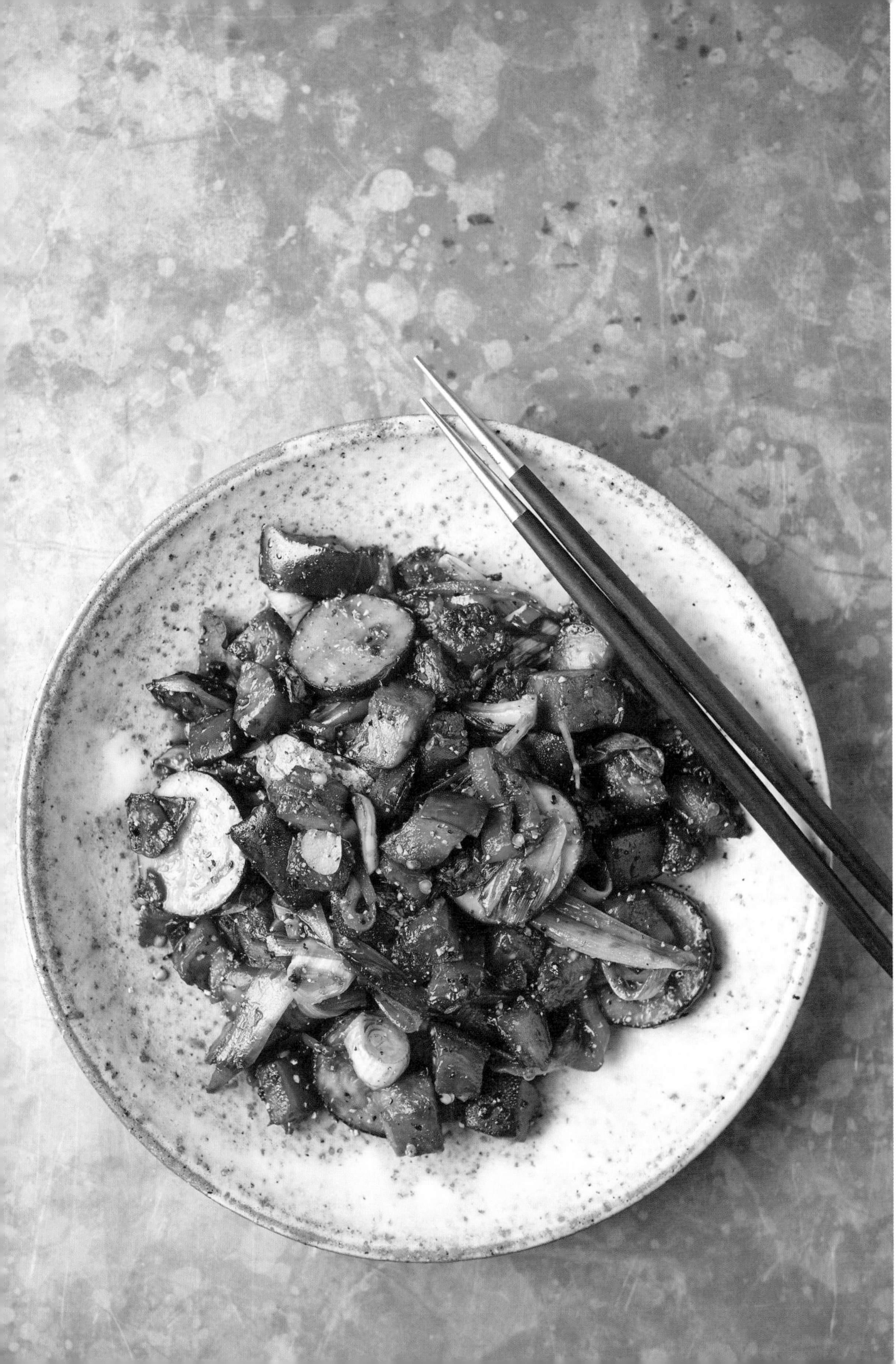

Macaroni Cheese Frittata

One of the ultimate images of comfort-food joy has to be the sneaky picking of the best bits. Whether it's lasagne or macaroni cheese, those charred, burnished bits that transform from tender, cheesy pasta to smouldered and crunchy corners are some of the most happiness-inducing nibbles we can encounter. This macaroni cheese frittata, with its burnished underside, is basically a giant crispy corner.

75g (2¾oz) macaroni

50g (1¾oz) evaporated milk

½ tsp English mustard

50g (1¾oz) grated Cheddar,
    plus extra to finish

40g (1½oz) Stilton, crumbled

Small handful of parsley, roughly chopped

3 large eggs

1 tbsp sunflower oil

Tabasco sauce

Fine sea salt and
    freshly ground black pepper

Serves 2-4

Bring a medium saucepan of well-salted water to the boil. Add the pasta and cook according to the packet instructions – normally about 8 minutes – until al dente. Drain.

Return the pasta to the pan and add the evaporated milk, mustard, Cheddar, Stilton and parsley. Set over a medium heat and stir until the cheese melts into the milk and coats the pasta. Remove from the heat and allow to cool for 5 minutes. Season with salt and pepper to taste. Add the eggs to the pan with the pasta and beat until well mixed.

Set a small deep-sided frying or sauté pan over a medium heat. Once the pan is hot, add the oil then the egg and pasta mixture, and reduce the heat to medium-low. Cover with a lid or a larger pan, and fry for 10–15 minutes until the frittata is set. Drizzle with Tabasco sauce, scatter over a little extra grated Cheddar and serve.

Fishcake Rosti

This is somewhat of a hybrid between a potato rosti and a fish cake – two of my favourite lunches. I use shop-bought, ready-cooked, peppered mackerel for this, and serve it with an equally peppery bed of rocket.

Makes 4

For the rosti

400g (14oz) Maris Piper potatoes, scrubbed clean

1 tsp fine sea salt

3 spring onions, finely sliced

1 tbsp non-pareil capers, roughly chopped

150g (5oz) peppered mackerel fillet, skin removed

1 large egg

½ tsp fine white pepper

60g (2¼oz) unsalted butter

To serve

150g (5oz) soured cream

Small handful of dill, finely chopped

1 tbsp wholegrain mustard

Rocket leaves (as much as you like), washed

4 pickled cucumbers, finely sliced

2 tbsp extra virgin olive oil

Sea salt flakes

Set the tea towel onto the worktop and grate the potatoes, coarsely, into the centre of it. Sprinkle over the salt, then draw together the edges of the tea towel, encasing the potato flecks in a tight package, and squeeze like there is no tomorrow. The excess water from the potatoes should trickle out – do this over the sink, obviously.

When the potatoes are fairly dry, add them to a bowl with the rest of the rosti ingredients except the butter – make sure you flake the mackerel into pieces. Mix until well combined.

Set a large frying pan over a high heat. Once the pan is hot, reduce the heat to medium and add the butter. Divide the rosti mixture into four. Squeeze each portion into a tight ball with your hands, then flatten into a fat disc. Place each disc into the pan and fry for 4–5 minutes per side, until crispy and browned.

While the rosti fry, mix together the soured cream, dill and mustard in a small bowl. Toss together the rocket and slices of pickled cucumber in another bowl, then dress with a little olive oil and salt.

Serve the rosti with a pile of rocket leaves, a dollop of the soured cream mix and a small handful of the pickled cucumbers.

dinner time

evening table

Colourful Dinnertimes

As a child, I loathed the idea and practice of eating together. I'm sure many kids do. It was a time of forced family, which I felt was more symbolic than meaningful. My stepfather would insist that we eat with a knife and fork in the correct hands. I detested that instruction. For a child, the exuberance of life is far more important than the mundanities of etiquette. But as I get older, I seem to long for those rules and traditions. Growing up, I suppose, is both liberating and imprisoning. On the one hand, I'm more able and willing to tell an agitating person to politely piss off, but on the other hand I crave structure and protocol.

Those family meals, though, were unquestionably burdensome to me. If my stepbrothers weren't hassling me, I'd be acting out for attention. I remember a particular endless summer evening when, crouched around a big stone slab in our garden that we used as an informal table, I flicked my spoon of ice cream toward my sister, but I was never much cop at hand–eye coordination. The scoop of vanilla hit my stepfather on his chest. Mum stifled a laugh while he withdrew my computer rights. I should apologise for that, so I'll do it now. I'm sorry. But it was funny.

Childhood can be a very lonely time, even when at a busy dining table. It was especially so for me, because around that time and table I was coming to terms with my sexuality. I thought I might be gay, but I didn't want to be. My stepbrothers made it quite clear what they thought of queers, and I worried that my parents would think the same. While some may find solace in family mealtimes, they only served to accentuate my feeling of solitude. The colour, fizz and vibrancy of dinnertime was like a candle. It flickered hauntingly, and quietly waned, unnoticed by the other revellers. I knew that one day my parents would be dead, my sisters would be nurturing their own offspring, and I would sit at a table, night after night, alone. I thought I would live in secret, a hermit hidden away, spoken of in whispered tones in local pubs. How wrong I was.

That isn't how my life has panned out – not so far, thankfully. And every day I am grateful for that. My perspective of 'family' has shifted, and it is now a much broader notion than I could ever have grasped as a kid loathing his sexuality. My family now consists of my hairy boyfriend and my genetically-challenged dog, Abel. We aren't a man, woman and 2.4 children, but we are a family. This is something I only understood very recently, as we trundled home after a boozy pub lunch and my handsome partner lit the fire. It was an awakening, which has brought forgiveness for those years of angst. And now, every time we sit down to eat, even though it may be a very quick stir-fry or fridge-foraged mess, I am grateful for my little family. And that gratitude has made the larger, more frantic family dinners a much more wholesome affair.

I want to dedicate this chapter to the youths (and some adults) who are afraid of who they are. Embrace it, because if you catch that fearsome wind in your sail with courage and pride, it will carry you to beautiful shores. If you don't, you will be lost at sea. You are wonderful, and you will be loved.

ABEL

Eritrean Pancakes with Lentil stew

Before I begin, this recipe has to come with a caveat: this isn't at all an authentic version, but is rather inspired by the classic Eritrean injera pancakes and lentil stew. The real version is something I had at the Blue Nile restaurant in Woolwich, which is run by the sweetest lady and her family, when I lived in London. It remains one of the best meals I've ever had; it was inexpensive and made with nothing other than love in the heart. In their version, both the stew and bread are cooked and fermented slowly, so this is my express take on the recipe.

For the lentil stew	¼ tsp ground nutmeg	Serves 4
2 tbsp sunflower oil	250g (9oz) dried red lentils	
1 onion, roughly chopped	1 litre vegetable stock	
1 large carrot, roughly diced	A small handful of fresh coriander,	
2 garlic cloves, minced	roughly chopped, to serve	
1 tsp ground ginger		
1 tsp chilli powder	**For the pancakes**	
1 tsp ground coriander	4 large eggs	
½ tsp paprika	125g (4½oz) wholegrain teff flour	
¼ tsp ground cloves	1 tbsp sunflower oil	
½ tsp ground allspice	Fine sea salt	

For the lentil stew, set a medium saucepan over a high heat and add the oil. Once the pan and oil are hot, reduce the heat to medium and add the onion and carrot. Fry, stirring occasionally, for 5 minutes, then add the garlic and spices and fry for a minute. Add the lentils and stock, bring to the boil, then reduce to a rapid simmer and cook, stirring occasionally, for 20 minutes, or until the lentils are tender.

Meanwhile, make the pancakes. Put the eggs and 225ml (8fl oz) water into a mixing bowl, then add the flour and 1 teaspoon of salt, whisking until you have a smooth batter.

Set a large, deep-sided frying or sauté pan over a medium-high heat. Rub the pan with a little oil, then add a generous ladleful of the batter, swirling the pan as you do so to evenly coat the base of the pan. Fry until the pancake top is littered with pinprick bubbles, then flip and fry for a few seconds more to cook through. Roll up the pancake and transfer to a plate to keep warm, then continue with the remaining batter.

When the lentils are tender, season to taste, top with fresh coriander and serve with the pancakes. The idea is to rip off pieces of the pancake and scoop the lentil stew onto it.

Saag Halloumi

This is based on the classic British–Indian staple of saag paneer, though with a little more emphasis on lightness and freshness. While you can guarantee you'll find me propped against the table in a curry house on a Friday night, devouring vatfuls of the original kind, it would be a little too indulgent for a midweek dinner. This home version uses halloumi instead of paneer – I find the saltiness of halloumi brings out so much more character in the spices.

Serves 2

2 tbsp olive oil

250g (9oz) halloumi,
    cut into 2cm (¾in) dice

1 onion, finely sliced

2 garlic cloves, minced

4cm (1½in) piece of fresh ginger,
    peeled and finely grated

1 tsp ground coriander

1 tsp ground cumin

1 tsp ground turmeric

½ tsp chilli powder

200g (7oz) cherry tomatoes, halved

250g (9oz) baby leaf spinach

Fine sea salt

Put 1 tablespoon of the oil into a large, deep-sided frying or sauté pan and set over a high heat. As soon as the oil shimmers, add the halloumi and fry, tossing frequently, for a few minutes until the cheese is deeply browned. Tip the halloumi into a bowl lined with kitchen paper, and return the pan to the heat, along with the remaining oil and the onion. Fry the onion, again tossing the pan very frequently or the onion will burn, until lightly charred and somewhat softened – though I like to retain a little bite in the onion to balance with the tender halloumi – about 4 minutes.

Add the garlic and spices to the pan and fry, tossing, for a minute, then throw in the cherry tomatoes and 3 tablespoons of water. Cover the pan and allow the tomatoes to bubble and break down, just until they only vaguely retain their rounded shape – albeit weathered and deflated – about 5 minutes. Do stir the pan frequently so nothing catches on the bottom.

Reduce the heat to medium, and stir the halloumi into the curry, which should be much drier by now. Add the spinach (usually in one or two batches, allowing each to wilt before adding the next). Once the spinach has wilted, remove from the heat, taste and season as required. Serve immediately.

135

Sausage, Fennel and Greek Yogurt Pasta

Whenever I use cream cheese as an accompaniment to pasta – which I do occasionally if ingredients and patience are in short supply – I shudder with embarrassment. What would my readers think if they could see me now? It's a dirty secret, and I eat in shame as I stand over the kitchen sink. But the older I get, and the more confident I become in my life choices, I wonder why anyone should feel ashamed or guilty about something that brings them both comfort and nourishment? And why should we, as cooks, cling so rigidly to a set of conventions that serve only to constrain our culinary liberty? I recently stumbled across a recipe by Greek chef Diane Kochilas in which she uses Greek yogurt to make a simple pasta sauce. It makes perfect sense: the starchy pasta water emulsifies into the yogurt, making a tangy sauce that clings to the pasta. This recipe shall be the bridge from which the fear of eating cream cheese pasta tumbles away.

Serves 2

4 Cumberland sausages

1 tbsp olive oil

1 small fennel bulb, finely sliced

1 tsp fennel seeds

Leaves from 2 rosemary sprigs

250g (9oz) short pasta (I like gigli)

100ml (3½fl oz) white wine

400ml (14fl oz) boiling water

75g (2¾oz) full-fat, thick Greek yogurt

Small handful of parsley, roughly chopped

30g (1oz) pecorino or Parmesan, finely grated

Fine sea salt and freshly ground black pepper

Before you heat the pan, squeeze the sausage meat out of the skins and into a bowl, breaking it into small chunks. Heat a large deep sided frying or sauté pan (one you have a lid for) over a medium-high heat and add the oil. When the oil shimmers from the heat, add the sausage bits, the fennel and fennel seeds and the rosemary and fry, stirring frequently, until the sausages are lightly browned and the fennel has softened.

Throw in the pasta, wine and boiling water and allow to come to the boil – don't worry if the pasta isn't completely covered by liquid. Pop the lid on and cook for 7 minutes. Uncover the pan and cook for a minute or so more, just until the pasta is al dente, then remove from the heat and stir in the yogurt, parsley and cheese. Season to taste and serve.

Pancetta, Parmesan and Pea Farfalle

A few years ago, one-pan pasta dishes were – and I hate this phrase to an unreasonable degree – bang on trend. So many of them, though, saw all the ingredients getting cooked together in the pasta water, then fished out, seasoned and mixed together. The results were nothing but soggy, insipid tomatoes floating around with waterlogged pasta. This recipe doesn't require any draining, because the water – what little is left of it – becomes the sauce, so everything that goes into the pan, stays in the pan. Because you are cooking at a high heat here, please try to be quick – give the recipe a read a few times before you get started. This combination may seem a childish one, but rest assured the addition of wine and rocket serve to elevate it to a more sophisticated realm.

1 tsp olive oil

140g (5oz) smoked pancetta
    or bacon lardons

1 banana shallot, finely sliced

125ml (4fl oz) dry white wine,
    plus a drop extra to finish

250g (9oz) dried farfalle

¼ chicken stock cube

100g (3½oz) frozen petit pois

100g (3½oz) rocket leaves,
    roughly chopped

50g (1¾oz) Parmesan,
    finely grated

4 tbsp double cream

Small handful of parsley,
    roughly chopped

Pinch of freshly grated nutmeg

Fine sea salt and
    freshly ground black pepper

Serves 2

Set a large frying or sauté pan (one you have a lid for) over a high heat. Once hot, add the oil, pancetta and shallot and fry, tossing regularly, for 3 minutes, until the shallot is soft and slightly charred.

Add the wine and allow it to bubble and almost entirely evaporate – about a minute – then add the pasta and 450ml (15½fl oz) water and crumble in the stock cube. It will look as though there isn't enough water to cover the pasta, but don't worry, that's perfectly all right. Cook for 6 minutes, stirring frequently, then add the peas and pop on the lid. Cook for another 3 minutes.

Once the pasta is cooked, remove the lid and turn the heat down to low. Add the remaining ingredients to the pan, and stir to coat everything well, then cook for a minute or two, just to allow the cheese to melt and the rocket leaves to wilt. Add a little extra splash of wine to lift everything and season to taste. Stir, then remove from the heat and serve.

Crab, Chorizo and Sherry Gnocchi

While sherry might remind most of us of their grandma's drinks cabinet or, better still, the enchantment of the Sunday trifle, it's a key ingredient in Spanish savoury cooking. Although this recipe isn't authentically Spanish, the combination of sherry and crab is one I tried in Santander on a college trip many years ago. While most students tucked into their burgers, I merrily enjoyed my sophisticated lunch. Though I was left with less beer money that day...

Serves 4

4 tbsp olive oil
500g (18oz) packet of
    potato gnocchi
2 banana shallots, finely sliced
100g (3½oz) chorizo ring,
    finely sliced
2 garlic cloves, finely sliced
75ml (2½fl oz) Manzanilla
    sherry
2 plum tomatoes,
    roughly chopped
200ml (7fl oz) chicken stock
100g (5½oz) cooked white
    crab meat
Small handful of parsley,
    roughly chopped
A squeeze of lemon juice

Heat a large, deep-sided frying or sauté pan over a high heat. Once the pan is hot, add half of the oil and reduce to a medium heat. When the oil is hot and starts to shimmer, add the gnocchi and fry, tossing occasionally, until they are golden and crispy. If the gnocchi start to burn, the pan is too hot. Tip the golden gnocchi onto a plate lined with kitchen paper and set aside until needed.

Return the pan to a medium heat, add the remaining oil and then add the shallots and chorizo. Fry, stirring occasionally, for 5 minutes until softened and slightly coloured, then increase the heat to medium-high and add the garlic. Fry for a minute, until the garlic smells strongly, then pour in the sherry and allow it to bubble and reduce until almost completely evaporated. Add the tomatoes and fry those for a good few minutes, stirring occasionally, until soft. Pour in the chicken stock and allow it to bubble until reduced by two-thirds, then remove from the heat. Add the crab meat, parsley and gnocchi, and stir to mix. Serve with a squeeze of lemon juice.

Lamb, Lemon and Oregano Tagliatelle

When I think back to a holiday we took on the Greek island of Zakynthos, it's the light and the aromas that warmly greet me. While whizzing around on a quad bike, every so often the blinding light transformed into dappled bursts on the winding roads, which we negotiated through woodlands of soapy pine. In the midday sun, bright and startling, fig trees offered the only solaces of shade and musky scent. But it was the oregano that I found most spellbinding; its fragrance permeated the heavy air as we climbed the mountains. On that holiday I had fried lamb chops with fresh oregano and lemon juice – a simple and classic flavour combination that works so well with the earthiness of wholewheat tagliatelle. The milk here may seem a curious addition, but it's this ingredient that curdles from the lemon's acidity and is then brought back together with the cold butter – and it must be cold – to form the silky sauce.

250g (9oz) lamb mince

Serves 2

2 garlic cloves, minced

1 tbsp finely chopped oregano

Zest and juice of ½ unwaxed lemon
(save the other half for serving)

2 tbsp extra virgin olive oil,
plus extra for drizzling

250g (9oz) wholewheat tagliatelle

500ml (17fl oz) lamb stock

100ml (3½fl oz) milk

15g (½oz) cold butter

Fine sea salt and black pepper

Put the lamb into a mixing bowl along with the garlic, oregano and lemon zest and juice. Mix together until more or less evenly combined.

Heat a large, deep-sided frying or sauté pan over a high heat. Once hot, add the oil and then add the lamb mixture and fry, stirring frequently, just for a minute. Add the pasta, stock and milk, and enough water to just cover the pasta. Bring the liquid to the boil, reduce the heat to medium-high, then cover the pan and cook for 10 minutes.

Once the pasta is tender, remove the lid from the pan. There should still be some liquid – a fairly muddy, confused puddle – in the pan. Increase the heat to high and boil the liquid until it is almost entirely evaporated, then stir in the cold butter until you're left with just a thick slick of sauce sticking the lamb to the pasta. Season to taste – go steady with the salt – and serve with extra olive oil drizzled on top.

139

dinner time

Chicken Pad Krapow

Purists please avert your gaze, because this isn't an authentic version of the Thai classic. Here I've used regular, large-leaf basil, rather than the holy or Thai basil that this recipe would ordinarily demand. That's simply down to supply – the more authentic herbs just aren't easy to come by for the everyday cook. If you happen upon holy or Thai basil while shopping, grab it and use that instead.

The key to this recipe is prep, heat and speed – do not turn your hob down at any point, just keep the contents of the pan moving with the wooden spoon and it will be glorious. Anything below a high heat just leaves a soggy, bland mush. If you can't find chicken mince, just use pork or turkey.

Serves 4

200g (7oz) basmati rice, rinsed

For the pad krapow
5 bird's eye chillies, roughly chopped
1 banana shallot, finely sliced
4 garlic cloves, sliced
1 tsp caster sugar

2 tbsp light soy sauce
1 tbsp fish sauce
1 tbsp oyster sauce
500g (18oz) chicken mince
Small handful of basil leaves (see introduction)
4 tbsp sunflower oil

Put the rice into a medium saucepan and cover with a 2cm (¾oz) layer of recently boiled water. Bring to a boil over the high heat, then reduce the heat to medium and cover the pan with the lid. Cook for 8 minutes, then remove the pan from the heat and leave the lid on so that the rice steams for a further 8 minutes.

While the rice cooks, do all the prep for the pad krapow: put the chopped chillies, shallot and garlic into one bowl, and the sugar and the soy, fish and oyster sauces into a separate small bowl. Have the chicken and basil handy.

Set the wok over a high heat and allow it to get very hot. Once hot, add the oil and throw in the chillies, shallot and garlic. Fry, stirring constantly, until everything smells so strong that it startles your senses – about a minute. Throw in the chicken mince and fry, stirring constantly with a wooden spoon to break it up, for a couple minutes further, until the chicken is cooked through.

To finish, throw in the sauce mixture, toss for just 30 seconds, then remove from the heat and stir through the basil, allowing it to wilt slightly. Fluff up the rice with a fork, place mounds onto plates, then spoon over the pad krapow. Garnish with basil and serve.

Drunk Thai Tagliatelle

The inspiration for this dish comes from the Thai favourite, drunk noodles – so-named thanks to its spicy, sobering properties. Normally it's made with classic rice noodles, but the trend in Thailand at the moment is to serve it with spaghetti. For me, the feeble strands of this pasta were a little too thin to purvey enough of the sobering sauce, but the texture and flavour was spot on. I found the thicker ribbons of tagliatelle to be a more successful combination.

Another diversion is the use of regular, Italian basil. Normally this dish would be made with holy basil, but it's rarely available here. You can, of course, find it in Asian supermarkets and online, but regular basil is just fine if that's the difference between you making this or not.

250g (9oz) dried tagliatelle

For the stir-fry
6 garlic cloves, minced
3 bird's eye chillies,
    roughly chopped
2 tbsp sunflower oil
8 king prawns, peeled
    and deveined

3 baby sweetcorn, sliced into thirds
Small handful of basil, torn
1 fresh lime, cut into wedges, to serve

For the sauce
4 tbsp oyster sauce
2 tbsp light soy sauce
2 tbsp dark soy sauce
2 tsp fish sauce

Serves 2

First cook the pasta. Bring a medium saucepan of water to the boil (don't add any salt – the soy will be salty enough), drop in the pasta and cook according to the packet instructions – usually 9 minutes – then drain.

While the pasta cooks, put the garlic and chillies into a small bowl and the oyster, soy and fish sauces into another small bowl.

When the pasta has cooked, put the wok over a high heat and add the oil. When the oil starts to smoke, add the garlic and chilli and fry, tossing, until the garlic just starts to colour. Throw in the prawns and corn and stir-fry until the prawns are cooked through.

Add the drained tagliatelle and sauces to the wok and fry for another minute, tossing all the ingredients together, then remove from the heat and scatter over the basil, giving the wok another toss to combine. Serve with lime wedges.

Tex-Mex Crispy Pork Rice

While this may not be a remarkably novel combination of flavours, I don't think you can beat a spicy rice stir-fry. The key here, and what amplifies this from familiar territory, is to slightly burn the bottom of the rice. Not only does this give a wonderful texture, but the subtle smokiness aligns well with the spice combination.

Serves 4

2 tbsp sunflower or rapeseed oil
1 onion, finely sliced
250g (9oz) pork mince
3 garlic cloves, minced
1 tsp celery salt
1 tsp chilli powder
1 tsp ground coriander
1 tsp ground cumin
1 tsp smoked paprika
1 tbsp tomato purée

400g (14oz) can black beans, drained
198g (7oz) can sweetcorn, drained
250g (9oz) ready-cooked brown rice

To serve
1 lime
2 tbsp soured cream
Handful of coriander, roughly chopped
1 avocado, diced

Heat a large, shallow casserole over a medium-high heat. Once the pan is hot, add the oil, onion and mince, and fry, stirring regularly, for 10 minutes. The onion should soften, and may even colour a little. Add the garlic, celery salt and spices and fry for 30 seconds, then add the tomato purée and 3 tablespoons of water. Fry for a minute, before adding the beans, sweetcorn and rice. Stir-fry for a minute to mix everything, then pat it all down into an even layer on the bottom of the pan.

Reduce the heat to medium and cook for 15 minutes, until the rice on the bottom of the pan is golden and crispy.

Serve with a squeeze of lime juice, blobs of soured cream, a scattering of coriander and a little chopped avocado.

Crispy Polenta Lamb with Asparagus and Radish Coleslaw

While a crispy-coated lamb steak can easily be eaten or nibbled while on the run (I speak from experience), it's the union here of salty, crunchy meat and the tangy and refreshing coleslaw that makes this dish. This is a dinner that deserves to be eaten at the table with a glass of chilled rosé.

For the lamb

4 lamb leg steaks

200g (7oz) fine polenta or cornmeal

50g (1¾oz) Parmesan, finely grated

2 large eggs, beaten

Olive oil, for frying

Fine sea salt and freshly ground
    black pepper

For the coleslaw

300g (10½oz) asparagus spears

1 large carrot

150g (5oz) radishes

3 tbsp extra virgin olive oil

1 tbsp lemon juice

1 shallot, very finely sliced

1 heaped tsp mayonnaise

Small handful of parsley, roughly chopped

1 fresh lemon, sliced into wedges, to serve

Serves 4

Put the lamb leg steaks between two pieces of cling film, spacing them out well, and bash with a rolling pin or meat mallet until evenly thin (you might need to do this in batches). Season both sides of the lamb with salt and pepper.

Put the polenta or cornmeal and Parmesan into a shallow bowl or deep-rimmed plate and the beaten eggs into another. Add salt and pepper, generously, to both bowls and mix. One at a time, dip the lamb leg steaks into the egg, coating well, then into the polenta. Repeat from the egg to the polenta again to double-coat the steaks for extra crispiness.

Heat a large frying pan over a medium-high heat. Once the pan is hot, add enough olive oil so there's about 5mm (¼in) depth on the entire base of the pan. When the oil is hot, add the steaks and fry for 3 minutes per side until golden brown and cooked through.

Meanwhile, for the coleslaw, cut the asparagus, carrot and radishes into thin slices using a speed peeler. Put into a mixing bowl and add the remaining ingredients. Stir together with a generous pinch of salt and pepper.

When the lamb steaks are cooked, serve one per person with a generous mound of coleslaw and a lemon wedge.

Moroccan-spiced Pan-fried Chicken and Chickpeas

This is one of those dishes that deserves to be unveiled at the table; its simplicity coupled with its scent renders diners to rapture. The spice blend, ras-el-hanout, is pretty ubiquitous now, and so should be available in larger supermarkets (and, of course, online).

Serves 4

6 chicken thighs, skin on, bone in
Sea salt flakes
2 tbsp sunflower oil
2 garlic cloves, finely sliced
1 tbsp ras-el-hanout spice blend,
    plus extra for sprinkling
50ml (2fl oz) dry sherry
400g (14oz) can chickpeas, drained
175g (6oz) dried apricots

400ml (14fl oz) chicken stock
A squeeze of fresh orange juice
2 tsp pomegranate molasses
Small handful of dill, roughly chopped

To serve
200g (7oz) couscous
400g (14oz) hot chicken stock

Put the chicken thighs into a mixing bowl, add 1 tablespoon salt and toss together to mix well. Set a large, shallow casserole over a high heat and add the oil. When the oil is hot, reduce the heat to medium, add the chicken thighs, skin-side down, and fry for 5 minutes. The chicken skin should be deeply golden but not burned. Flip the chicken over and fry for 3 minutes on the other side.

Add the garlic and ras-el-hanout to the pan, tucking in the slices of garlic in between the chicken pieces. Throw in the sherry and allow it to bubble and hiss, until it has evaporated almost entirely. Add the chickpeas, apricots and chicken stock and allow to come to the boil. Reduce to a rapid simmer and cook for 20 minutes, ensuring the liquid reduces but doesn't entirely evaporate – if the pan dries out, add a splash of water.

Meanwhile, put the couscous into a mixing bowl and pour over the hot chicken stock. Cover with cling film or a plate while the chicken cooks.

When the chicken is cooked through and the liquid is scant, remove from the heat. Squeeze over a drizzle of orange juice and pomegranate molasses, sprinkle over the dill and finish with a scatter of sea salt flakes.

Uncover the couscous and season to taste. Serve alongside the chicken.

Hot Chicken Caesar

Much as I love the cooling crunch of crisp baby gem in a Caesar salad, there's a lot to be said for griddled lettuce. A dear friend once taught me that cookery is all about concentration of flavours. She was exactly right, and that principle rings true here; in griddling the lettuce the flavour is intensified beyond belief. Although a Caesar dressing ordinarily uses a mixture of olive and vegetable oils, I just can't resist the brassica tones of a saffron-yellow rapeseed oil, so that's what I use. If you wish to lean more toward tradition, feel free.

Serves 2

For the salad	For the dressing
1 thick wedge of sourdough bread, cut into 2cm (¾in) cubes	1 large egg yolk
Extra virgin olive oil, for drizzling	1 tbsp lemon juice
1 baby gem lettuce, cut into 6 wedges	½ tsp English mustard
350g (12¼oz) chicken mini fillets	5 anchovies, from a jar, finely chopped
Fine sea salt and freshly ground black pepper	1 small garlic clove, minced
	60g (2¼oz) rapeseed oil
	50g (1¾oz) Parmesan, flaked

Set a griddle pan over a high heat and allow it to get ferociously hot. Meanwhile, put the cubes of sourdough into a mixing bowl and drizzle generously with extra virgin olive oil. Add a pinch of salt and toss together until well coated. Griddle the bread cubes for a minute or so per side, until charred and crispy. Remove the bread from the pan and place onto a serving platter.

Add the lettuce wedges to the bowl and drizzle with a little oil. Add salt and toss together. Put the lettuce wedges onto the hot griddle pan and fry for a minute or so per side until wilted and charred. Arrange, with the bread, on the platter.

Season the chicken in the bowl with a little more olive oil and salt, then fry it on the hot griddle pan for 3 minutes per side, or until cooked through and lightly charred. Arrange the chicken on the platter and allow to rest.

Wash the mixing bowl out well – ensuring there's no chicken residue whatsoever on it. Add the egg yolk to the bowl along with the lemon juice, mustard, anchovies and garlic. Whisking continuously, add the rapeseed oil a drop at a time. If you add it too quickly, you won't emulsify the fats, which is the aim here. When you've added about two-thirds of the oil, you can pour in the rest in a very thin stream while you continue to whisk. Once you have a light but thick sauce, stop whisking.

Drizzle the sauce over the salad, and finish with some large flakes of Parmesan and season.

a flash in the pan

Pan-fried Sea Bass with Cashew, Coconut and Cavolo Nero Salad

Sea bass is such an easy fish to cook - it's quick and so simple to prepare. The salad here is fresh and sharp, and pairs so well with the fish. I remember when I first made this, it was the during the heatwave of 2018 when the air was thick with smoke from the local grasslands which were ablaze with wildfire.

For the salad

100g (3½oz) coconut flesh, finely sliced

100g (3½oz) cashew nuts

100g (3½oz) mangetout, thickly shredded

100g (3½oz) cavolo nero, thickly shredded

1 tbsp runny honey

2 tbsp lime juice

1 tbsp light soy sauce

2 tsp fish sauce

Fine sea salt

For the sea bass

2 sea bass fillets, skin on

50g (1¾oz) plain flour

50g (1¾oz) unsalted butter

1 tbsp white rice vinegar

Serves 2

Heat a large, deep-sided frying or sauté pan over a high heat. Once the pan is hot, add the coconut and cashew nuts and fry, tossing, for a minute or so until the nuts are lightly coloured. Add the mangetout and a splash of water and fry for a minute, then throw in the cavolo nero and fry, tossing occasionally, until the cavolo nero is warmed through. Tip into a large mixing bowl.

In a small bowl, mix together the honey, lime juice, soy and fish sauces and a pinch of salt; pour this dressing into the bowl with the cavolo nero and stir to coat everything.

Slice shallow slashes into the skin of the sea bass, about 1cm (½in) apart. Dust just the skin side with flour and fine sea salt. Return the pan to a medium heat and add the butter. When the butter melts and starts to sizzle, place the sea bass into the pan, skin-side down. Hold the fillets in place for a few seconds to stop them curling up. Fry for 3–4 minutes, until most of the flesh has turned a ghostly white, with just a streak of pinkish grey on the top. Flip the fillets over and fry for a further minute on the other side.

When the fish is cooked, remove it from the pan, then deglaze the pan with the white rice vinegar, swirling it into the pan juices. Pour the liquid over the fish.

Serve the sea bass with a handful of the tangy, sweet salad.

Frying Pan Lasagne

I'm not one for gimmicks when it comes to food, and 'skillet lasagne' is something I have grimaced at time and time again on social media. On trying it, however, I was an instant convert. Granted, it doesn't have the towering depth of a baked lasagne, but what it lacks in size it makes up for in convenience and flavour. You might be surprised here that I don't brown the beef and pork mince, but I find doing so far too often toughens the meat. With this method the meat stays absolutely tender.

Serves 4

2 tbsp olive oil

1 onion, finely chopped

1 tsp fennel seeds

3 garlic cloves, minced

100ml (3½fl oz) red wine

2 x 400g (14oz) cans cherry tomatoes

1 beef stock pot

1 tsp dried oregano

250g (9oz) beef mince

250g (9oz) pork mince

8 dried lasagne sheets, broken
   into shards

125g (4½oz) mozzarella, torn into chunks

Fine sea salt and freshly ground black pepper

For the topping

1 tsp olive oil

50g (1¾oz) fresh breadcrumbs

2 tbsp finely chopped parsley

For the ricotta

175g (6oz) ricotta

Zest of ½ unwaxed lemon

Put a large, deep-sided frying or sauté pan over a high heat and add the oil. Once the oil is hot and starts to shimmer, add the onion and fennel seeds and fry, stirring, for a couple of minutes until the onion is slightly coloured and softened.

Add the garlic and fry for a few seconds, then throw in the wine and allow to bubble and almost entirely evaporate. Add the tomatoes, 200ml (7fl oz) water and stock pot, and allow to come to the boil, then add the oregano, beef and pork. Stir to mix everything well, then add the lasagne – it's important to dot the sheets around the pan, to avoid any sticking together as they soften.

Allow the pan to come to the boil, then reduce the heat to medium-high, pop on the lid and cook for 5 minutes. After this time, remove the lid and cook for a further 10–15 minutes, stirring occasionally to avoid any bottom-burning, until the sauce is thickly reduced. Add the torn mozzarella, salt and pepper – about a teaspoon of each – and stir to mix everything well.

While the sauce bubbles, heat a small saucepan over a medium heat. Add the olive oil and breadcrumbs. Fry, tossing occasionally, just until the breadcrumbs are toasted – about 3 minutes. Remove from the heat and toss in the chopped parsley.

In a small bowl, beat the ricotta with the lemon zest and a generous pinch of salt and pepper.

To serve, scatter the breadcrumbs on top of the lasagne, and serve with generous blobs of the lemon ricotta.

Bloody Mary Prawn Tacos
with Celeriac and Lime Slaw

While the Bloody Mary cocktail, like Marmite, may be a severely polarising thing, this permutation is sure to please most. The tender prawns are so well suited to the spicy tomato sauce, and the celeriac slaw offers both earthiness and acidity to complement and cut through it all. With the mayonnaise, I use the Kewpie brand (which I use in the Okonomiyaki recipe on page 67) – but if all you have is the regular variety, that'll be fine.

For the prawns

1 tbsp sunflower oil

1 banana shallot, finely sliced

1 celery stick, finely sliced

2 garlic cloves, finely sliced

½ tsp celery salt

50ml (2fl oz) vodka or white wine

½ tsp Tabasco sauce

1 tsp horseradish sauce

1 tsp Worcestershire sauce

150ml (5fl oz) tomato juice

500g (18oz) king prawns,
    peeled and deveined

1 tbsp parsley, finely chopped

Freshly ground black pepper

For the celeriac slaw

100g (3½oz) celeriac, peeled

1 tbsp lime juice

½ tsp celery salt

Small handful of coriander, finely chopped

To serve

4 flour tortillas

Mayonnaise (use the Kewpie brand, if possible)

2 fresh limes, cut into wedges

Makes 4

Set a large frying pan over a high heat. Once the pan is hot, add the oil, shallot and celery. Fry for a minute until everything starts to sizzle, then reduce the heat to medium. Fry, stirring occasionally, for about 10 minutes, until the shallot is just softened. If the shallot starts to catch, reduce the heat further.

When the shallot is soft, increase the heat to high and add the garlic and celery salt. Fry for a minute then throw in the vodka or white wine and allow the alcohol to bubble and evaporate almost entirely. Add the Tabasco, horseradish, Worcestershire sauce and tomato juice and bring to the boil, then throw in the prawns. Fry just until the prawns are cooked through, then remove from the heat and stir in the parsley and a good grinding of black pepper.

For the celeriac slaw, coarsely grate the celeriac into a mixing bowl. Add the lime juice, celery salt and coriander.

To serve, fill the tortillas with the slaw before layering with the prawns. Top with a squeeze of mayonnaise and serve with lime wedges and extra slaw.

Lamb Loin and Smoked Aubergine Yogurt

Smoked aubergine dip is manna from heaven, transforming even the driest of flatbreads into a most gratefully received purveyor of this edible joy. It was only when my dear friend John Gregory-Smith wrote his book Turkish Delights *that I heard of Ali Nazik – smoked aubergine yogurt topped with spiced lamb. In his version, John uses lamb mince, and it's divine. I've opted here for something a little more expensive: lamb loin fillets, which when sliced, lie atop the smoky sauce with real juiciness. The only caveat to this recipe, and one I should draw your attention to before you set off to buy the ingredients, is that you need a gas hob because the aubergine is cooked directly on the flame. If you don't have one, it could be cooked under a hot grill and turned occasionally, until the skin is completely blackened, but you won't get quite the same flavour.*

Serves 4

For the lamb

1 tbsp tomato purée

1 tbsp finely chopped
    oregano leaves

¼ tsp hot chilli powder

2 lamb loin fillets

1 tbsp sunflower oil

40g (1½oz) unsalted butter

Fine sea salt and freshly
    ground black pepper

For the yogurt

1 large aubergine

300g (10½oz) Greek yogurt

1 garlic clove, minced

Small handful of parsley, roughly chopped

Seeds from 1 pomegranate

Sliced warm pita breads, to serve

Put the tomato purée into a mixing bowl along with the chopped oregano, the chilli powder and ½ teaspoon each of salt and pepper. Mix to combine, then add the lamb and coat well.

Set a large frying pan over a high heat with the sunflower oil. Once the oil is hot, add the lamb and sear on all sides until deeply browned. Then fry the lamb, rotating the fillets constantly in the pan, for 6 minutes. Add the butter to the pan and allow it to melt with a fierce sizzle, then spoon the melted butter over the lamb fillets. Set the cooked lamb onto a plate and allow to rest, covered with foil.

Set the gas hob to a high flame. Pierce the aubergine multiple times with a fork, and place it directly onto the flame. Cook until each side is blackened and blistered – only turn the aubergine when the side touched by the flames is ready. Set aside until cool enough to handle, then remove the blackened skin and discard. Chop the flesh finely, with a generous pinch of salt and pepper. Add to a mixing bowl with the yogurt and minced garlic. Taste for seasoning, adjusting if necessary.

Spread the aubergine mixture onto a large plate. Slice the lamb thinly and scatter it over the aubergine. Finish with a sprinkling of freshly chopped parsley and pomegranate seeds. Serve with slices of warm pita bread.

first bites

food to wake
up to

A Ghost Creeping up the Stairs

As we start to stir in our beds and our heart rates speed up, the scent of toast creeps up the staircase. It sneaks through the crack under the door, into the chambers where daylight itself fears to tread. Alarms may have chimed for hours, muted by a disgruntled finger, not rousing the souls whose cheeks caress the bedsheets.

That aroma is one of the few things that can easily resurrect the deepest of sleepers. As a little boy, I remember hearing terrifying sounds coming from the kitchen first thing, which would jolt me awake. Then, satisfied that it was just Mum, I'd nestle down and drift back to sleep, soon to be woken by the smell of toast: haunting homeliness.

It's within that first hour or so of waking that we present ourselves in the rawest form. Our hair is scruffy and unkempt, our teeth unclean. We have not yet mustered the willpower to don our masks and be who we want to be – we are, instead, who we are. There isn't the pomp or ceremony of dinnertime; that has crumbled away to expose the truest versions of ourselves. It follows that the people with whom we can bear to have breakfast, in our rawest form, are people who are more likely to remain in our lives.

Surely that in itself calls for some sort of celebration? This chapter is somewhat of a paradox because these recipes, while still quick to throw together, are comparatively slow. Most breakfasts these days comprise little more than cereal and toast, and so the recipes here are far more indulgent. They are more of a celebration – something to enjoy with the scruffiest morning members of your tribe, the ones who know you the best.

You may wonder why I have saved this chapter until last. I have pondered for years the answer to what would be my last meal. I always assumed I'd want something pillowy, like a pizza, or as extravagant as an Indian banquet lasting for days. But on reflection, what I would truly want is to be around the people I love the most. I'd want to wake up to that haunting smell of toast; to the clatter of pots and pans beneath my floorboard; to my tribe waiting for me around the table.

Greek Yogurt Panna Cotta with Pistachios, Pomegranate and Cranberries

Although this does require an overnight stint in the fridge, this is still a very rapid dish to put together. And what's more, I find that the knowledge of a ready-prepared breakfast sitting in my fridge only serves to lull me deeper to sleep. Many people will avoid this recipe because it contains gelatine, and that is something they aren't used to using. But trust me when I tell you not to be nervous about this ingredient, the panna cotta is ridiculously simple to make.

Serves 4

For the panna cotta

3 gelatine leaves
 (I use Dr Oetker platinum grade)
300ml (10fl oz) whole goat's milk
3 tbsp honey
Zest of 1 unwaxed lemon
400g (14oz) Greek yogurt

To serve

25g (1oz) pistachios, roughly chopped
40g (1½oz) dried cranberries
40g (1½oz) pomegranate seeds
2 figs, quartered
1 tbsp runny honey

Fill a pint glass with cold water from the tap. Add the gelatine leaves, one at a time so they don't stick together, ensuring they are fully submerged. Leave to soak for 5 minutes.

Put the milk, honey and lemon zest into a medium saucepan. Set the saucepan over a medium-high heat and allow the milk to come to a simmer. Once it does, remove the pan from the heat. Retrieve the gelatine leaves from the water and squeeze out all of the excess moisture. Add the leaves to the pan of milk and stir to dissolve them. Allow the milk to cool slightly, then whisk in the Greek yogurt until the mixture is even and smooth. Pour the mixture into a shallow casserole or ceramic roasting dish. Place it into the fridge and allow it to set overnight.

In the morning, scatter the top of the panna cotta with pistachios, cranberries, pomegranate seeds and the fig quarters. Drizzle over the honey and serve up, letting everyone scoop out a good spoonful of panna cotta and fruit.

Burnt Butter, Pecan and Apple Miracle Granola

I'm not one for undue hyperbole, so when I say this is a miracle recipe, please do believe me. There's little more gleefully welcomed to a breakfast table than homemade granola, but the oven-baked variety, while so simple, is a little time-consuming. This is made within a matter of minutes, and the seeds and dried fruit can be adjusted to suit personal tastes. If you are vegan, you could substitute the butter with coconut oil, but I much prefer burning the butter to get that caramelised hit. When made, this will keep in an airtight tub or jar for weeks – if you ensure the hole in the jar is small enough to restrict pilfering handfuls.

200g (7oz) jumbo porridge oats
70g (2½oz) pecans, roughly chopped
70g (2½oz) pumpkin seeds
70g (2½oz) buckwheat
60g (2¼oz) unsalted butter
60g (2¼oz) maple syrup

60g (2¼oz) light brown muscovado sugar
100g (3½oz) dried apple, roughly chopped
½ tsp ground cinnamon

Makes 10 servings

Preheat a large frying pan over a high heat. Once the pan is hot, add the oats and toast, tossing frequently, for a minute or two. Pour the oats into a bowl, return the pan to the heat and add the pecans, pumpkin seeds and buckwheat. Toast, tossing frequently, for 2 minutes, until everything smells wonderfully roasted and the pumpkin seeds have stopped popping violently. Pour into a separate bowl.

Put the pan back on the heat and add the butter, allowing it to melt and sizzle, until the sizzling stops and you have a thick foam made of fine bubbles on top – this will only take a minute or two. It should be burnt, so don't be flapping. Just throw in the syrup and sugar, and heat for a minute, stirring to combine everything well, letting them bubble together. Ensure there are no lumps of sugar lurking about in the pan.

Add the oats to the pan and stir to coat them really well in the sweet, caramelised butter mixture. Once well coated, allow them to cook for just a minute more, stirring constantly. Pour the oats onto a baking sheet and allow to cool for a few minutes, then toss together with the toasted nuts, seeds and buckwheat, the dried apple and the cinnamon.

Once completely cool, tip into a large storage jar.

Lemonade Griddle Pan Waffles with Lemon and Rosemary Butter

Impatient urges, while best associated with demanding children, still do creep up on me sometimes. When I was last in New York, staying with a dear friend, we had a last supper at Sweet Chick on the Lower East Side. Accompanying my fried chicken was a filthy pile of waffles, stacked oh-so-high with a pale yellow butter gently melting, threatening to tumble over the cliff of pillowy waffles. That butter, sweetened with icing sugar and spiked with lemon and rosemary, was beautiful. This was a recipe I wrote immediately on my return.

Serves 4

For the waffle batter
250g (9oz) self-raising flour
5g (¼oz) bicarbonate
  of soda
10g (½oz) caster sugar
5g (¼oz) salt
175ml (6fl oz) cloudy lemonade
200ml (7fl oz) whole milk
2 large eggs
Spray oil, for greasing

For the lemon and rosemary butter
125g (4½oz) unsalted butter, at room temperature
Zest of 1 unwaxed lemon
½ tbsp fresh rosemary, finely chopped
2 tbsp icing sugar, plus extra to dust

Preheat a griddle pan over a low-medium heat – this seems a little premature, but if your griddle pan is anything like mine, it takes a good while to heat up.

For the batter, simply toss together the flour, bicarb, sugar and salt in a mixing bowl – it helps to give it all a whisk to blend everything together. In a jug, beat together the lemonade, milk and eggs until well mixed. Whisking the dry ingredients well and constantly, pour a little of the liquid ingredients into the bowl – it's far easier to get any lumps out while the batter is still fairly thick, so work at it before adding all of the liquid. Once you have a smooth batter, stop mixing – you don't want to break down the proteins in the flour, as these cause gluten to form, and then your waffle will be tough and chewy rather than fluffy and tender. Let the batter rest while you make the butter.

Put the ingredients for the butter into a bowl and beat until pale and fluffy – I use a hand-held electric whisk for ease, but there is something fulfilling (if not exhausting) about using a wooden spoon and elbow grease.

Spray the griddle pan really well with oil – or, pour oil into it and carefully wipe it around the pan with some kitchen paper. Add the batter to the pan and allow it to fry for 6 minutes or so, until most of the batter is fairly set and there are many pinprick bubbles on top of the waffle.

Time to flip. This will make a bit of a mess, it'll most likely end up down your cupboard fronts and trouser legs, but cupboards can be wiped and clothes can be washed – you won't get this waffle any other way. I find the easiest way to flip is to slide it onto a large plate or chopping board, invert the pan over the top, then flip the pan and plate together so the waffle falls back into the pan, uncooked side down. Fry for a further 4 minutes, until bouncy and set all the way through.

Divide the waffle into four and serve on plates with a generous knob of the lemon and rosemary butter on top. Dust with extra icing sugar, if you're feeling particularly greedy.

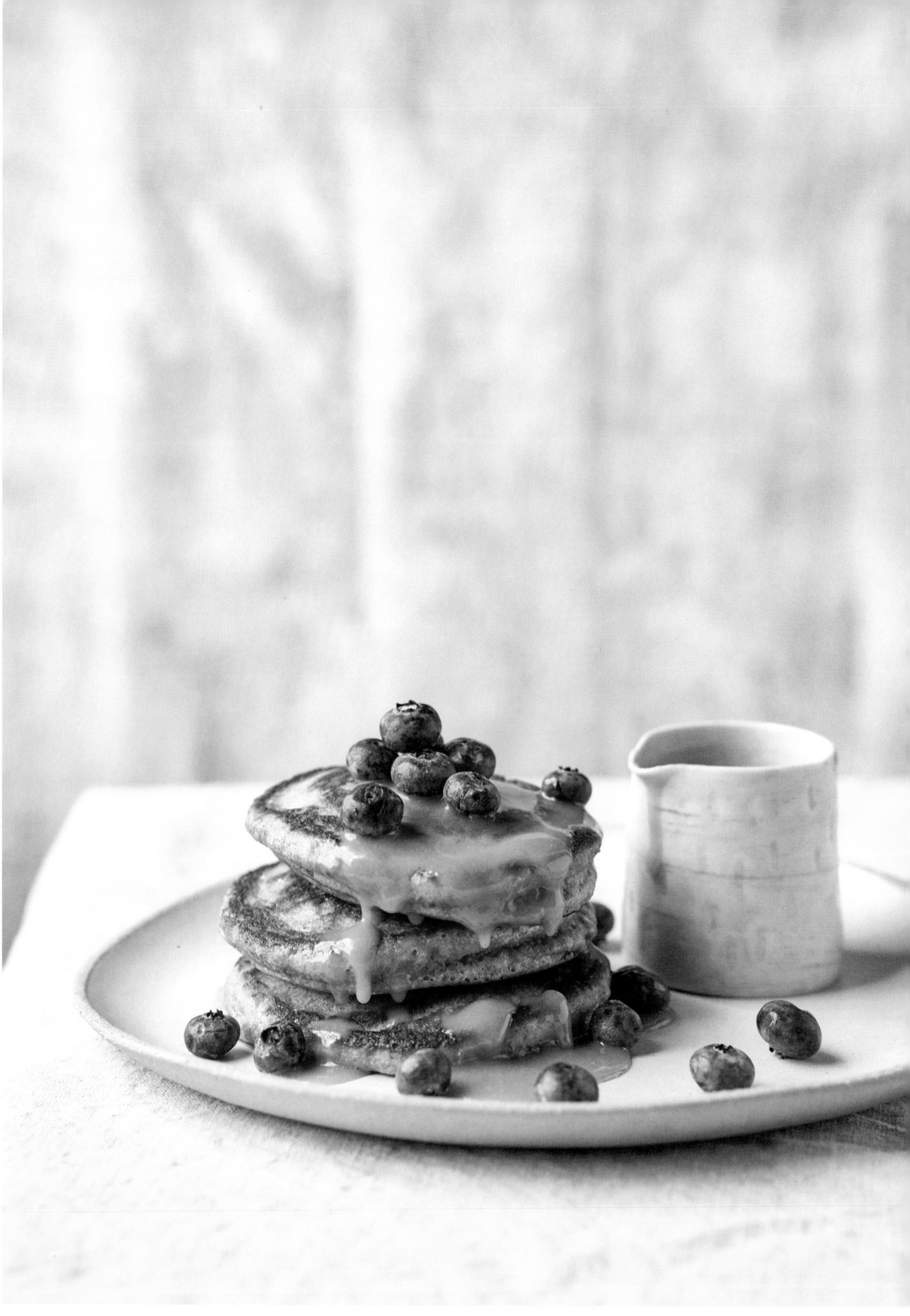

Tahini and Honey Pancakes

While pancakes ordinarily command a simply sweet finish to accompany them, I find they often lack a more complex combination of flavours. These deliver on all fronts. The pancakes themselves, made from wholemeal flour, are slightly nutty and wholesome, and the tahini-honey sauce is the perfect balance of nutty, sweet, earthy and bitter.

For the pancake batter	To serve	Serves 4
225g (8oz) self-raising wholemeal flour	4 tbsp runny honey	(makes 8 pancakes)
½ tsp fine sea salt	4 tbsp tahini	
4 large eggs	2 tbsp hot water	
2 tbsp runny honey	100g (3½oz) blueberries	
4 tbsp tahini		
125ml (4¼floz) whole milk		
30g (1oz) butter, for frying		

For the pancake batter, put the flour into a mixing bowl with the salt. Put the eggs, honey and tahini into another bowl and whisk together until smooth, then whisk in the milk. Gradually pour the liquid ingredients into the dry, whisking constantly until you have a very thick but smooth batter.

Heat a large frying pan over a high heat and, once the pan is hot, reduce the heat to medium-high and add the butter. When the butter has melted, ladle in the batter to create pancakes of about 10cm (4in) in diameter. Fry until pinprick bubbles form on the top (1–2 minutes) then flip and fry for a further minute. Once cooked, stack the pancakes on a plate to keep them soft and warm.

In a small bowl, whisk together the honey, tahini and hot water into a fairly runny sauce. Drizzle this over the pancakes and finish with the blueberries.

Marmalade Brulée French Toast

Much as I love French toast – and I seriously, utterly do – I sometimes wish its flavour was a little more developed. This recipe realises exactly that wish, although it was born from hangover clumsiness. Promising my partner French toast one morning after a few cocktails, I mistakenly put the bread in the toaster. Not wishing to waste it, I used it for the French toast anyway. We were grateful for that mistake.

Serves 1

2 slices of thick white bread
1 tbsp tangy marmalade
1 large egg
2 tbsp milk
50g (1¾oz) unsalted butter
2 tbsp icing sugar

Start by toasting the bread, and toast it well – the stronger the flavour, the better the end result. Spread one piece of toast with marmalade, and sandwich together with the other slice.

Put the egg and milk into a shallow bowl and whisk together vigorously until well combined. Dunk the toast into the sunny yellow liquid, soaking each side for about a minute.

Meanwhile, preheat a large, deep-sided frying or sauté pan over a medium heat. When the pan is hot, add the butter and allow it to melt. Add the sandwich and fry, gently, for 3–5 minutes per side, or until each side is seriously golden and crispy.

Remove the toasted sandwich from the pan and set onto a plate. Dust liberally with icing sugar, then using a chef's blowtorch, burn the sugar to a blackened, animal print pattern. Allow the brulée crust to set, then eat in whichever way you feel fit: with cutlery, with hands, with face plant.

173

Brunch Burritos

Those who adore the savoury punch of the full English breakfast will relate to this oh-so-piquant little number. Imagine the spiciness of chorizo along with the tenderness of baked beans, all bundled together in a crispy wholemeal tortilla. I don't think I need to say much more here, other than – what are you waiting for?

2 wholemeal tortillas	4 large eggs	Makes 2
100g (3½oz) chorizo picante, sliced	100g (3½oz) Manchego or	
100g (3½oz) chestnut mushrooms,	Cheddar, grated	
finely sliced	2 tbsp olive oil	
1 medium leek, finely sliced		
½ courgette, finely sliced	**To serve**	
200g (7oz) can baked beans	1 tbsp finely chopped fresh chives	
Knob of unsalted butter	4 tbsp soured cream	

Set a frying pan over a high heat. Once hot add the tortillas, one at a time, and warm each for just 10 seconds or so per side. Stack them up, and cover them with an inverted plate to keep them warm and soft.

Return the pan to a medium-high heat and add the chorizo, mushrooms, leek and courgette. Fry, tossing occasionally, for 5 minutes, until the chorizo has leaked out its spicy juices and the vegetables are ever so slightly softened. Add the baked beans, stir through, then remove from the heat.

Set a saucepan over a medium heat. Once hot, add a knob of butter and allow it to melt. Break the eggs into a bowl and beat together, add to the pan and cook until perfectly scrambled – as sloppy or as firm as you prefer, though a little firmer will make the assembly easier.

To assemble the burritos, put a quarter of the bean filling mixture onto the centre of each tortilla, along with a quarter of the cheese and the scrambled egg. Fold the top and bottom sides of the tortilla over the filling, then repeat with the left and right sides, encasing the filling completely in a little bundle. Place them, seam-side down, on a chopping board.

Wipe the pan out, and set it over a medium-high heat. Add the oil, and once it is hot, add the tortillas, seam-side down. Fry for a few minutes per side, until golden and crispy. Stir the chopped chives into the soured cream in a little bowl and serve alongside the burritos for dunking.

Fried Eggs, Potato Rosti and Infused Maple Syrup

No, I haven't gone mad; this weird and wonderful creation – fit for any time from brunch to supper – is all about the contrasts of flavour and texture. The sweet maple syrup is balanced with the earthy, salty rosti, and the crunch of the potatoes is softened by the silky egg yolk. And who needs an excuse to add bacon? It shouldn't work, but it really does.

Serves 2

For the syrup
100g (3½oz) maple syrup
1 tsp mustard seeds
1 thyme sprig
1 garlic clove, peeled

For the rosti and bacon
450g (1lb) Maris Piper
  potatoes
Fine sea salt
6 rashers smoked
  streaky bacon
50g (1¾oz) unsalted butter

For the eggs
50g (1¾oz) unsalted
  butter
2 tbsp sunflower oil
4 large eggs

For the infused maple syrup, put everything into a small saucepan and set over a medium heat. Once the maple syrup is warm, reduce the heat to low and leave to infuse while you prepare everything else.

To make the rosti, grate the potatoes coarsely (as long as the skin is clean, there's really no need to peel them). Put the grated potatoes onto the centre of a tea towel and sprinkle, generously, with fine salt. Toss together, then bring the edges of the tea towel up to meet each other, like making a dim sum, trapping the potato inside. Squeeze firmly over the sink to expel the excess moisture from the potatoes.

Heat a large frying pan over a medium-high heat. Fry the bacon for a few minutes per side or until at the desired level of crispiness. Transfer to a plate and keep warm, then return the pan to the heat and add the butter. Divide the potato mixture into four, shape each portion into a ball, then flatten into a rough disc. Fry the rosti for 3–5 minutes per side, until deeply golden and very crispy. Set the cooked rosti onto another plate and keep warm.

Return the frying pan to a slightly hotter heat and add the butter and oil. When the butter has melted and starts to sizzle, crack the eggs into the pan and fry for a few minutes, until the whites have set and the yolks are still runny – it helps to spoon some of the hot fat over the eggs as they fry, to set the upper egg white.

Serve the eggs and bacon on top of the rosti, and drizzle as generously as you feel necessary with the infused maple syrup.

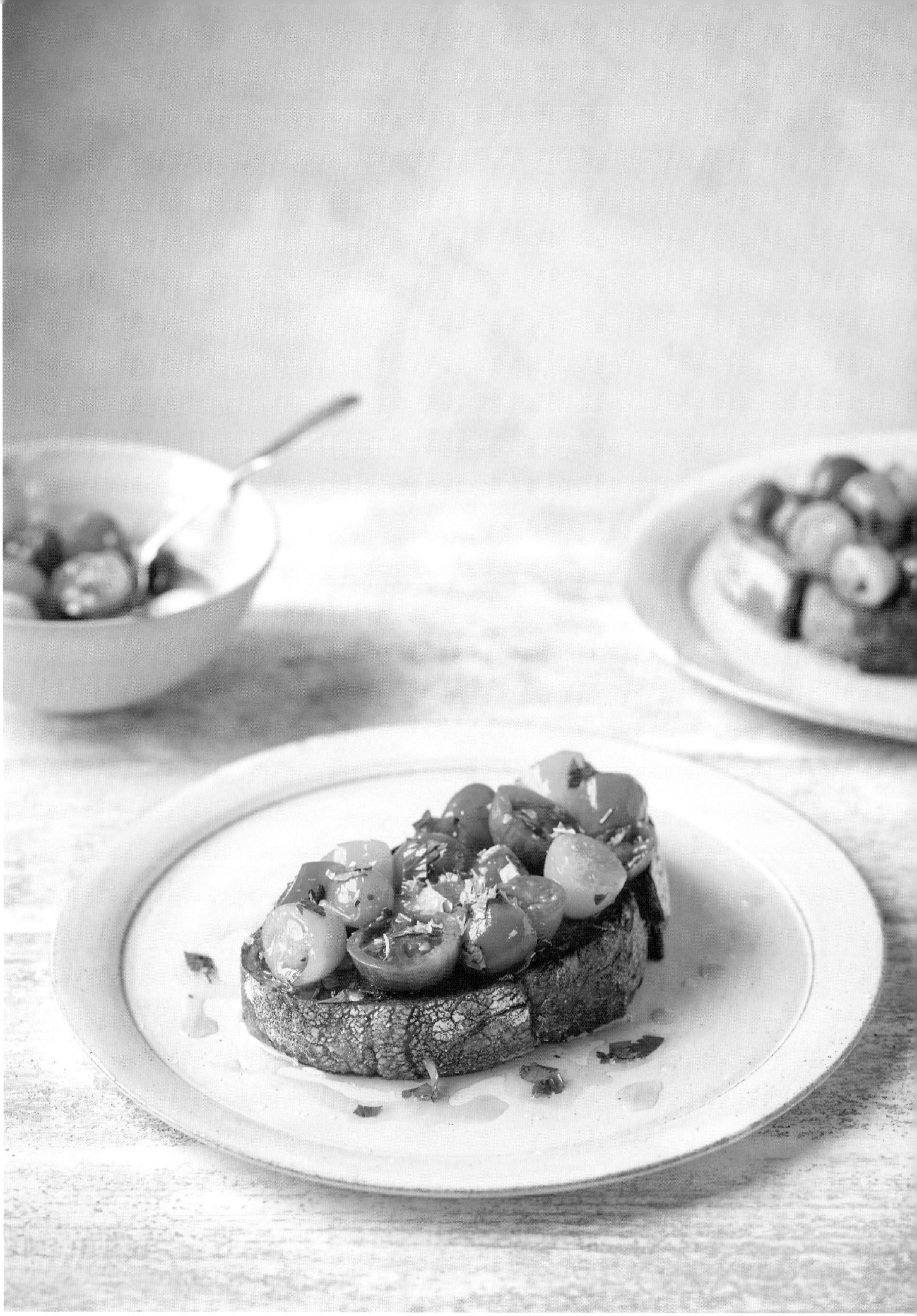

Breakfast Bruschetta with Confit Tomatoes and Garlic

This is an adaptation of my focaccia recipe in my book Perfect Plates in 5 Ingredients. *In that recipe, I infuse oil with tomatoes and garlic to drizzle over the focaccia. When I recently made the focaccia for a friend's party, I absentmindedly left the oil at home. Not wishing to throw it away, I later scooped out the tomatoes with a slotted spoon and had them on toast as the perfect breakfast. The leftover infused olive oil can also be saved and reused to drizzle on salads – just pass the oil through a sieve lined with a piece of muslin to get rid of any bits.*

100ml (3½fl oz) extra virgin olive oil

200g (7oz) mixed cherry
   tomatoes, halved

4 garlic cloves,
   peeled and lightly crushed

Small handful of parsley,
   roughly chopped

Sea salt flakes and
   freshly ground black pepper

2 thick slices of sourdough toast

Serves 1-2

Set a medium saucepan over a high heat and add the oil, tomatoes and garlic. Allow the oil to heat up until the tomatoes start to sputter. At this point, reduce the heat to low, add the parsley and season and allow everything to infuse together for 25 minutes.

With a slotted spoon, scoop everything out of the oil and serve on slices of toast.

Coffee and Cornflake French Toast

Cornflake French toast might seem a bit of a gimmick, but it's a marvel. While the flavour is somewhat subtle, the added crunch to that pillowy soft bread is where the virtue lies. I've taken this a step closer to breakfast perfection with the addition of coffee, but if you're a coffee-phobe, feel free to leave it out.

Makes 4 slices

3 tbsp whole milk

2 tsp instant espresso powder

1 tbsp runny honey

2 large eggs

50g (1¾oz) cornflakes

50g (1¾oz) unsalted butter

4 thick slices of brioche

Maple syrup, to serve

Put the milk and espresso powder into a mixing bowl and whisk to combine. Add the honey and eggs and whisk until well mixed.

Crush the cornflakes roughly – some should be fine powder, while other pieces should be fairly chunky. Tip into a wide bowl or plate.

Set a large frying pan over a medium-high heat. Once the pan is hot, reduce the heat to medium and add the butter, swirling it around the pan to melt.

Dunk the brioche slices, one at a time, into the egg mixture, pressing them down gently to soak them well. Dip both sides of the brioche slices into the cornflakes to coat completely, then pop into the pan. If your pan is big enough, fry all four pieces at once, otherwise cook the brioche in batches, only dipping and coating them just before frying. Fry over a medium heat for 3–4 minutes per side, until deeply golden and crispy.

Serve with a drizzle of maple syrup.

Full English Shakshuka

Shakshuka, the traditional Tunisian dish of eggs poached in a spiced tomato sauce, has been hugely popular among UK food writers for a good few years. Its savouriness is the perfect antidote to a delicate disposition, and it is sure to leave you fulfilled. This version marries that spicy original with the wonders of the English breakfast. A part I wouldn't skip here is the fried bread; not only does it soak up all of the excess fat from the bacon, but you're going to want to dunk something crunchy into that glorious pool of tomato and yolk.

1 tbsp sunflower oil	½ tsp cumin seeds	Serves 1-2
2 pork sausages	200g (7oz) can baked beans	
80g (3oz) smoked bacon lardons	200g (7oz) passata	
2 thick slices of sourdough	2 large eggs	
1 banana shallot, sliced	Fine sea salt and freshly	
5 chestnut mushrooms, thickly sliced	ground black pepper	
1 garlic clove, finely sliced	Tabasco sauce, to serve	
½ tsp smoked paprika		

Set a medium, deep-sided frying or sauté pan over a medium-high heat. Once the pan is hot, add the oil, sausages and bacon. Fry, stirring the bacon and turning the sausages occasionally, until the bacon is crispy and the sausages are deeply browned – a good few minutes per side.

Put the bacon and sausages onto a small plate and set aside until needed. Put the sourdough slices into the pan – still on the heat. Fry on each side in the meaty oil until golden brown and crispy. Remove from the pan and set aside.

With the pan still over a medium-high heat, add the shallot and mushroom slices, with a generous pinch of salt. Fry, stirring frequently, for a few minutes until the mushrooms are soft and the shallot is lightly coloured. Add the garlic, paprika and cumin and fry, stirring, for a minute. Add the beans and passata and stir to combine. Return the sausages and bacon to the pan, then reduce the heat to low and simmer, covered, for 5 minutes.

Make two wells in the tomato sauce and crack in the eggs. Cover and poach for 3–5 minutes, until the whites are set but the yolks are still runny. Serve immediately with pepper and Tabasco sauce, and the sourdough toast for dunking.

Scandi Mackerel on Pumpernickel

Fish for breakfast reminds me of my stepfather. Although not much of a cook, he always makes his own boiled kippers (mostly, I think, because my mother can't stand them). I'm partial to a bit of fish at breakfast time, too, and while I can't face the startling strength of kippers, I could eat mackerel from dawn until dusk. The apple, celery and capers in this mixture serve as a perfect acerbic foil against that tender and smoky fish.

Serves 2

4 large slices of pumpernickel

1 Granny Smith apple, finely diced

1 celery stick, finely sliced

2 tbsp mayonnaise

1 tbsp capers, roughly chopped

150g (5oz) smoked mackerel, flaked

A few fronds of dill

1 radish, finely sliced

Sea salt flakes

Lemon wedges, to serve

Toast the pumpernickel bread in a toaster for a minute or two per side – it'll turn just slightly crispy, but will remain mostly moist.

In a mixing bowl, mix together the apple, celery, mayonnaise, capers and mackerel. Spread, pile or scoop the mixture onto the toasted pumpernickel. Scatter over dill, radish slices and sea salt flakes. Serve with lemon wedges.

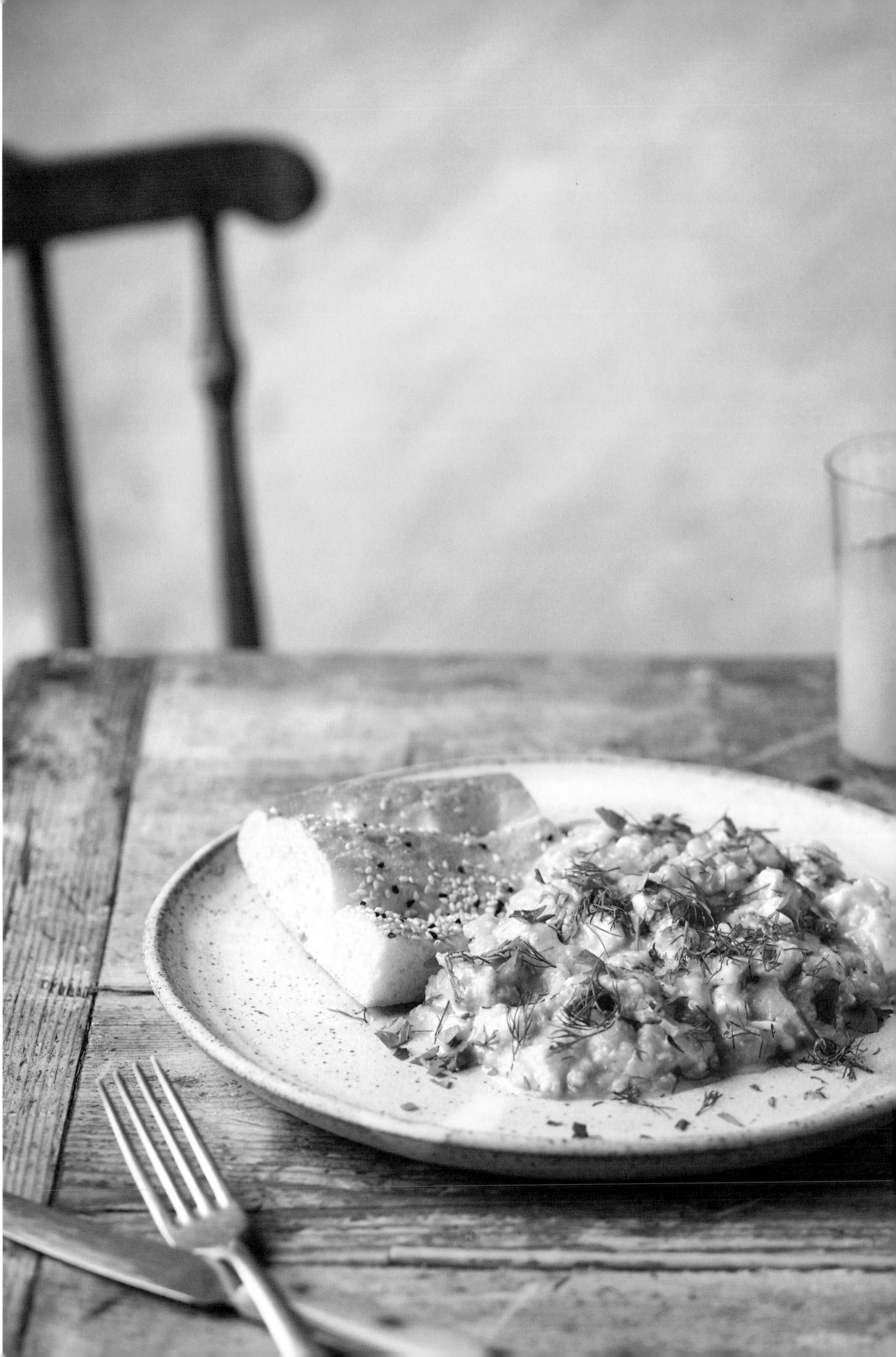

Persian Eggs on Toast

This is the Iranian method for scrambled eggs, and it is something I had a few years ago at a fabulous pop-up restaurant in London. I make this so often for breakfast – and sometimes for dinner, too. There's really nothing to this recipe, as long as you cook everything gently, and resist overcooking the eggs.

2 tbsp olive oil
200g (7oz) feta, crumbled
Pinch of dried thyme
4 large eggs, beaten
½ tsp ground turmeric
Freshly ground black pepper

To serve
4 portions of Turkish flatbread
1 tbsp roughly chopped parsley
1 tbsp roughly chopped dill

Serves 2-4

Set a large, deep-sided frying or sauté pan over a medium-high heat and add the olive oil. When the oil shimmers, reduce the heat to medium and add the feta cheese and thyme. Fry, stirring, until the feta is melting. Reduce the heat to low and add the eggs and turmeric. Fry, stirring and scraping the eggs off the bottom of the pan, just until the eggs are set but still fairly runny – if you like them a little firmer, that's up to you. Season with pepper to taste – there's probably no need for any extra salt, thanks to the feta.

Serve the eggs with the Turkish flatbread, and scatter over the parsley and dill.

Masala Scrambled Eggs with Naan Toast

This is a particularly savoury breakfast, but one I have come to crave morning after morning. The eggs are gently spiced and slightly salty, the naan is pillowy and sweetened by the mango chutney, and everything is brought together with the onion, coriander and tamarind. If you can't find tamarind anywhere, use lemon juice – it won't be the same, but it'll bring the refreshing acidic bite needed to round it all up.

Serves 2

For the eggs

4 large eggs

1 tsp fine sea salt

½ tsp fine black pepper

½ tsp ground cumin

½ tsp ground coriander

½ tsp ground turmeric

½ tsp nigella seeds

Knob of unsalted butter, for frying

To serve

2 naan breads (garlic naan is delicious here)

2 tsp mango chutney

1 small red onion, finely sliced

Small handful of coriander, roughly chopped

1 red chilli, finely chopped

1 tsp tamarind concentrate
  (I use the Natco brand)

Sea salt flakes

Put a large frying pan over a high heat. Once it's hot, add the naan breads, one at a time, frying for about 30 seconds per side, until warmed through. Pile them on a plate, then invert another plate on top to keep them warm and soft.

In a mixing bowl, beat together the eggs, salt and spices until very well combined.

Return the pan to a medium-high heat and add the butter. Once the butter melts and starts to sizzle, add the eggs. It's important to keep the eggs moving, scraping them off the bottom of the pan with a spoon or spatula constantly. When the eggs look as though they've thickened but still have a little movement to them, put them back into the mixing bowl you used to beat them – don't worry, the residual heat in the eggs will cook any raw egg that was left in the bowl.

Spread the mango chutney over the naan breads and top with the eggs. Finish with a scattering of onion, coriander and chilli, a drizzle of the tamarind and a few flakes of sea salt.

Index

U.S. Glossary

Aubergine – eggplant
Bicarbonate of soda – baking soda
Caster sugar – superfine sugar
Coriander – cilantro
Cornflour - cornstarch
Courgettes – zucchini
Custard – vanilla pudding
Dark brown/light brown muscocado sugar – dark brown/light brown sugar
Double cream – heavy cream
Frying pan - skillet
Gelatine - gelatin
Golden syrup – light corn syrup
Icing sugar – confectioners' sugar
Plain flour – all-purpose flour
Polenta - cornmeal
Pudding – dessert
Self-raising flour – self-rising flour
Spring onions - scallions
Wholemeal flour – wholewheat flour